PRESSURE
COOKER
COOKBOOK

PRESSURE COOKER COOKBOOK

Home-cooked meals
in 4 minutes

Dale Sniffen

I would like to dedicate my first book to my lovely wife Lorraine, partner in food and my business accountant. To my two sons: Hayden for his adventurous palate and Byron for his brutal honesty while recipe testing—both keep me striving for culinary perfection!

To all my pressure cooking students; their unrelenting demand for something different keeps me constantly developing and creating new recipes.
Thank you all.

CONTENTS

Fate led Dale Sniffen and I to meet ten years ago. While happily grocery shopping, I spotted him demonstrating his skill in a mall. I watched him ply his trade—cooking in front of an attentive crowd, using fresh ingredients and a simple recipe. Then I tasted his fare and was convinced: I had found 'my' chef.

A few years and many highly successful cooking demonstrations and classes later, I presented Dale with his first 'new generation' pressure cooker. As expected, he embraced pressure cooking with a passion and developed many new, award-winning recipes. The applause at the end of every class demonstrated his students were convinced that pressure-cooked dishes are convenient to prepare as well as delectable and delicious, courtesy of Dale's love of cooking, his profound knowledge of food and his amazing creativity.

I know you'll be pleasantly surprised by the results you'll achieve when you create dishes for your friends and family using Dale's recipes. Not only will they love you for the superb cuisine you present to them, they'll line up in anticipation of the next culinary chapter.

Thank you, Dale, for turning simple dishes into a feast and for turning Australia on to pressure cooking again. And thank you for helping me stay in love with the craft of pressure cooking, following a 40-year devotion.

— Chantal Roger
General Manager
Pressure Cooker Centre

INTRODUCTION

I was first introduced to a pressure cooker by my good friend and food lover Carmelo Mussca in the 1980s. My wife and I went to his house and he whipped up the best octopus I've ever tasted, cooked in a pressure cooker in less than six minutes. From that moment on I was fascinated with pressure cooking.

A pressure cooker is a wonderful utensil for creating tasty, home-cooked meals in a short amount of time. It uses boiling water inside a tightly sealed chamber to create steam. The steam is trapped inside the cooker, creating a high-pressure environment that quickly breaks down the fibres of the food yet retains all the natural flavours. With a small amount of prep work, you can easily create delicious meals—lamb, veal and beef shanks, stocks, vegetables, soups, curries, breads, cheesecakes, puddings and many others—in a fraction of the time traditional cooking methods take. The electric pressure cooker is even easier, exemplifying the term 'new and improved'!

I've been teaching pressure cooking for more than 20 years. This book is a collection of my favourite pressure cooking recipes, which my students had success with in their very first attempts. In this busy world, fresh home-cooked food is often replaced with less healthy options.

I hope this book inspires you to realise the full potential of the pressure cooker. 'Let the food do all the work!'

Thanks for reading!

— Chef Dale Sniffen

BASICS

COOKING WITH A PRESSURE COOKER

Normally, water boils at about 100°C (212°F). In a pressure cooker, the pressure increases the boiling point to about 120°C (250°F). At this temperature food, like meats, potato and hard vegetables, tenderises in about one-third of the time of conventional cooking methods. The result is better flavour and more nutrition in one-third of the time. Today's pressure cookers are easy to use, safe and fast; they let the food do all the work.

The recipes in this book are for both stovetop and electric pressure cookers. The functions for electric pressure cookers vary, but many have sauté, steam and warm settings, with low, medium and high pressure variables. I have given instructions for both types of cookers, but in most cases, where a recipe states low temperature for a stovetop pressure cooker, a low pressure setting on an electric pressure cooker is appropriate. Always check your instruction manual for specific settings. Following are some tips for using your pressure cooker.

- **Use enough liquid so the pressure can build**
  Up to four cups is enough.

- **Don't fill the pressure cooker more than two-thirds full**
  It's important to leave room for the steam to build up and create pressure, as well as for the food to expand. If you overestimate the cooking liquid, remove the contents and naturally reduce the liquid or use a thickening agent. (Remember you can only fill the pressure cooker two-thirds of the way.) Thicken your meal at the end of the cooking process; don't add thickening agent into the pressure cooker as the food will scorch on the bottom very quickly.

- **Brown meat in small batches**
  Overcrowding the pressure cooker can result in the meat stewing in its own juices, which gives the dish a flavourless, undercooked taste.

- Cooking times start when you get to pressure

- Check the manual for all care instructions
  For example, some lids should not be immersed in water, just wiped with a damp cloth before storing.

- Store the pressure cooker with the lid upside-down on the pot
  Locking the lid on before storing can damage the rubber seal, and doing so while wet can make it impossible to open and attract mould.

- How to clean a scorched pressure cooker
  If you do scorch the bottom of a pressure cooker, half fill it with water and one lemon, cut in half. Apply high heat with the lid on and pressure cook for 15 minutes. Use the natural release method to release the pressure. Open the lid and scrape the bottom with a flat wooden cooking spoon to remove the burnt items. Empty out the cooker and scrub the bottom clean.

  To avoid scorching invest in a diffuser, especially if you're using a gas ring. A diffuser reduces the heat by 20 per cent.

RELEASING PRESSURE

There are several ways to release the pressure during and after the cooking process, and each recipe includes the best method for that dish.

- Natural release method
  Remove the pressure cooker from the hot burner and let the pressure drop by cooling down naturally at room temperature. I use this when making stocks, soups, rice and risottos.

- Quick release water method

  For stove top pressure cookers remove the pressure cooker from the stove, place it in the sink and gently run cold tap water over one-third of the lid until steam dissipates and the pressure indicator lowers. All new pressure cookers have a safety feature where you will not be able to open the lid until all pressure has been fully released. If you can't open it there is still pressure in the cooker. Allow more cold water to run over one-third of the cooker and open the steam release valve to quickly release the pressure.

- Automatic release method

  Remove the pressure cooker from the stove. Turn the pressure selector dial to the 'release' position and the steam will release automatically. I use this method with electric pressure cookers as the water method can't be used.

NOTE

In this book:

- Most recipes serve between 6 and 8 people

- All recipes are based on using 15 psi pressure

TECHNIQUES AND TIPS

DOUBLE BROWNING

When you reduce meat juices after the first browning, the meat starts to brown again. This removes the rawness of the meat and gives the dish that nice roasted flavour.

REFRESHING

This term refers to lowering the temperature of the food as quickly as possible in order to stop the cooking process. Place the food under cold running water or in a large bowl of ice water until it is completely cold.

THICKENING AGENTS

To thicken 1 litre (2 pints) cooking juices:

Classic roux	3 tablespoons plain (all-purpose) flour mixed with 3 tablespoons butter
Packet thickening	5 tablespoons gravy powder whisked into a paste
Gluten-free	200g (7oz) red lentils, cooked for 20 minutes
Natural reduction	Remove meats and slowly reduce to a sauce consistency

* **Gluten-free thickening method**
  I recommend using 'rice slurry'. To make slurry, measure out 1½ cups rice flour in a mixing bowl. Add 1 cup cooking juices and whisk until combined. Slowly pour the slurry into the simmering cooking juices, whisking until the desired thickness is reached.

PARTS AND UTENSILS

- A typical electric pressure cooker essentially consists of a removable, non-stick bowl and lockable lid (1).
- Electric pressure cookers include several digitally-controlled settings, including sauté and steam settings (2).
- The main pressure release valve, usually located on the handle (3).
- A complete kit may include spatulas, ladels and measuring cups (4).

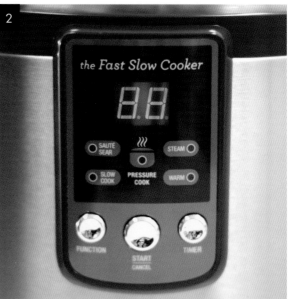

- A trivet (5) is a thin metal frame that holds the stainless steel steaming tray (6) above the water (7–8).
- An extra safety release window is located on the edge of some pressure cooker lids. Please check your instruction manual on the specifics of your particular pressure cooker.
- Always check your owners manual for the safety features your pressure cooker offers.

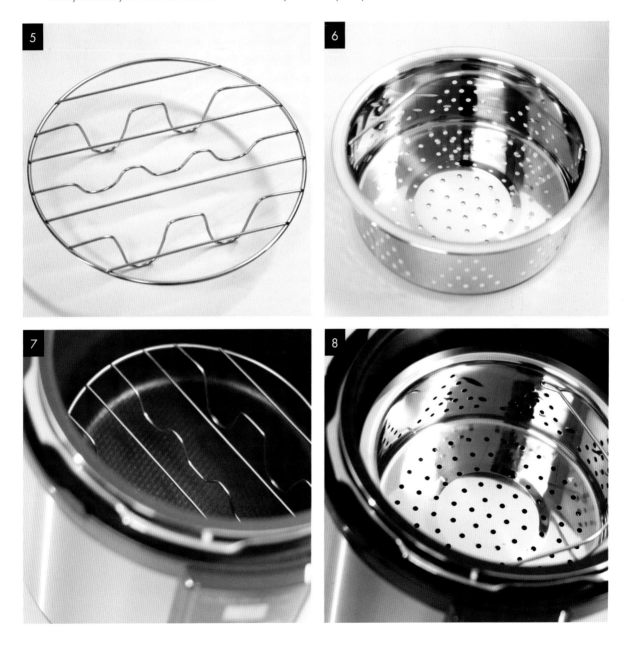

ccan red lentil
uinoa spinach
agus split pea
m minestrone
horizo chicker
le leek potato

STOCKS
AND
SOUPS

STOCKS AND SOUPS

BASIC STOCK AND SOUP

You can't go past a good homemade stock; it is the foundation of many meals. Today, it is difficult to find time to create a stock from scratch. However, pressure cookers can produce a basic vegetable stock in 15 minutes and chicken stock in 30 minutes. It's quick, easy and you know what's in it. You'll never look back to store-bought stock.

DOS AND DON'TS OF PRESSURE COOKER STOCKS

Do:

- Prepare large, roughly cut pieces of vegetables: celery hearts cut into quarters, brown onions peeled and cut into quarters, leeks split in half and carrots, unpeeled, split in half and then half again
- Use quality fresh vegetables and herbs
- Use low heat when you get to pressure

Don't:

- Cut your vegetables too small
- Add green celery leaves; they are too bitter
- Use high heat; this will make your stock cloudy

SEAFOOD STOCK

Preparation time:	10 minutes
Pressure cooking time:	6 minutes
Pressure release:	Natural release method

1 brown onion, cut into quarters

1 celery heart, cut into quarters

2 carrots, split, cut into batons

500g (1lb) prawn shells

1 whole salmon frame, cut into
  four pieces

2 ripe tomatoes, sliced

2 bay leaves

Add all ingredients to the pressure cooker, along with 4L (8 pints) water. Lock the lid in place.

Stovetop: Apply medium to high heat to achieve the seal and allow pressure to build up. Once high pressure is reached, turn to low heat and cook for 6 minutes.

Electric: Set to low pressure and cook for 6 minutes.

Use the natural release method to slowly release the pressure.

Strain the stock through a fine sieve, discarding bones, shells and vegetables.

Freeze in plastic containers for later use.

Great for risotto, soups and pasta sauces.

BEEF STOCK

Preparation time:	1 hour
Pressure cooking time:	1 hour
Pressure release:	Quick release water method

1.5kg (3lb) beef stock bones or ox
    tails, prepared by the butcher
2 large brown onions, peeled and
    roughly chopped into quarters
2 celery hearts, quartered
2 split unpeeled carrots, cut in half
6 garlic cloves, whole
3 tablespoons olive oil
3 large ripe tomatoes, diced
6 stalks flat-leaf parsley
2 bay leaves
4 tablespoons sea salt
1 tablespoon whole peppercorns

Preheat oven to 200°C (400°F).

Evenly scatter bones in a large, heavy-based roasting tray. Roast, uncovered, for about 40 minutes, or until the bones are well browned. Turn occasionally.

Drain off excess fat and deglaze pan with 500ml (1 pint) water, scraping down caramelised beef juices.

Meanwhile, preheat pressure cooker to medium heat or to sauté setting.

Sauté vegetables and garlic in olive oil until fragrant. Add 4.5L (9 pints) water, roasted beef bones and deglazed juices, tomatoes, herbs, salt and pepper. Allow stock to simmer. Skim off any fat impurities that rise to the surface. Lock the lid in place.

Stovetop: Apply medium to high heat to achieve the seal and allow pressure to build up. Once high pressure is reached, turn heat to low and cook for 1 hour.

Electric: Set pressure to high. Once high pressure is . reached, turn to low pressure and cook for 1 hour.

Use the quick release water method or quick release lever to release the pressure.

Allow stock to cool slightly before straining through a fine sieve. Discard ingredients.

Freeze in plastic containers for later use.

BASIC CHICKEN STOCK

Preparation time:	10 minutes
Pressure cooking time:	30 minutes
Pressure release:	Quick release water method

2kg (4lb) chicken carcass or chicken
  necks, washed
2 medium brown onions, peeled
  and cut into quarters
2 celery hearts, quartered
2 split unpeeled carrots, cut in half
2 vine-ripened tomatoes, cut in half
2 bay leaves
5 stalks flat-leaf parsley
5 sprigs fresh thyme (optional)
1 tablespoon black peppercorns

Place washed chicken bones in pressure cooker. Add 4L (8 pints) water and bring to the boil.

Simmer for 5 minutes, skimming any fat impurities that rise to the surface.

Add all prepared vegetables, herbs and peppercorns. Lock the lid in place.

Stovetop: Apply medium to high heat to achieve the seal and allow pressure to build up. Once high pressure is reached, turn to low heat and cook for 30 minutes.

Electric: Set pressure to medium. Once high pressure is reached, turn to low pressure and cook for 30 minutes.

Use the quick release water method or quick release lever to release the pressure.

Strain the chicken stock through a sieve and discard the contents.

Freeze in plastic containers for later use.

BASIC VEGETABLE STOCK

Preparation time:	10 minutes
Pressure cooking time:	10 minutes
Pressure release:	Natural release method

3 tablespoons grapeseed oil
or olive oil

2 medium-sized brown onions,
peeled and cut into quarters

2 celery hearts, quartered

2 medium-sized split carrots,
cut in half

4 vine-ripened tomatoes, sliced

6 Swiss brown mushrooms

4 bay leaves

½ bunch flat-leaf parsley

Few sprigs of thyme leaves

1 tablespoon celery salt

1 tablespoon whole
black peppercorns

Heat oil in pressure cooker. Add onion, celery hearts and carrots. Sauté vegetables well until they just start to brown. Add 4L (8 pints) water, tomatoes, mushrooms, herbs, salt and peppercorns and allow to simmer briefly. Lock the lid in place.

Stovetop: Apply medium to high heat to achieve the seal and allow pressure to build up. Once high pressure is reached, turn to low heat and cook for 10 minutes.

Electric: Set pressure to high. Once high pressure is reached, turn to low pressure and cook for 10 minutes.

Remove pressure cooker from the heat and set aside until pressure is released. Strain and discard ingredients.

Freeze in plastic containers for later use.

SMOKED BACON AND PUMPKIN SOUP

Preparation time:	15 minutes
Pressure cooking time:	12 minutes
Pressure release:	Natural release method

2 large brown onions,
  finely chopped
6 stalks celery, chopped
1kg (2lb) Kent or Japanese
  pumpkin, peeled and
  roughly diced
6 garlic cloves, crushed
4 tablespoons olive oil
300g (10oz) smoked
  bacon bones
3 tablespoons concentrated
  tomato paste
3L (6 pints) chicken or vegetable
  stock (see pages 24–25)
1½ cups (300g, 10oz) red lentils
2 bay leaves
Sea salt, to taste
White ground pepper, to taste
Nutmeg, to taste
1 cup (250g, 8oz) sour cream
Chives, chopped, to garnish
Crusty bread, to serve

Preheat pressure cooker to medium heat or use sauté setting.
    Sauté prepared vegetables and garlic in olive oil
for 3 minutes. Add bones and tomato paste. Sauté for another
3 minutes. Deglaze with stock and bring to a slow simmer.
    Sprinkle lentils on top of the soup, followed by bay leaves.
Lock the lid in place.
    Stovetop: Apply medium to high heat to achieve the
seal and allow pressure to build up. Once high pressure is
reached, turn to low heat and cook for 12 minutes.
    Electric: Turn to medium pressure and cook for 12 minutes.
    Use the natural release method to release the pressure.
    Remove the lid and discard bacon bones. Season with
sea salt, white pepper and a good pinch of nutmeg. Add sour
cream. Puree soup with a stick blender until smooth.
    Garnish with chopped chives and serve with crusty bread.

MOROCCAN RED LENTIL AND QUINOA SOUP

Preparation time: 10 minutes
Pressure cooking time: 5 to 7 minutes
Pressure release: Quick release water method

2 brown onions, chopped
6 cloves garlic, crushed
3 tablespoons olive oil
4 stalks celery, chopped
2 carrots, diced
2 tablespoons Moroccan and curry
    blend (see Sauces and Spices)
3 tablespoons concentrated
    tomato paste
2 tablespoons preserved lemon,
    chopped or zest of ½ a lemon
3 waxy unpeeled potatoes, diced
    (Nadine or Kepler are
    good varieties)
400g (14oz) dried red lentils
100g (3½oz) red quinoa
4L (8 pints) vegetable stock (see
    page 25), or water
3 coriander roots, leaves reserved
    to garnish
2 bay leaves
Sea salt and white pepper, to taste
2 cups (500g, 1lb) fresh cherry
    tomatoes, chopped

Preheat pressure cooker on medium heat or use sauté setting.
    Sauté onion and garlic in olive oil until fragrant.
    Add celery, carrots and spice blend. Sauté for 2 minutes or until fragrant. Add tomato paste, preserved lemon, potatoes, lentils, quinoa, stock, coriander roots and bay leaves. Simmer for a further 2 minutes. Lock the lid in place.
    Stovetop: Apply medium to high heat to achieve the seal and allow pressure to build up. Once high pressure is reached, turn to low heat and cook for 5 to 7 minutes.
    Electric: Turn to medium pressure and cook for 5 to 7 minutes.
    Use the quick release water method or quick release lever to release the pressure.
    Season with salt and pepper to taste. Garnish with chopped tomato and fresh coriander leaves, chopped. Coriander may be substituted with dill or flat-leaf parsley.

SPINACH AND ASPARAGUS SOUP WITH SMOKED SALMON

Preparation time:	15 minutes
Pressure cooking time:	6 minutes
Pressure release:	Quick release water method

4 tablespoons olive oil

2 tablespoons butter

1 brown onion, roughly chopped

3 bunches fresh asparagus spears,
   bottom third peeled,
   roughly chopped

3 royal blue potatoes, peeled
   and diced

2L (4 pints) vegetable stock
   (see page 25)

½ bunch English spinach leaves

Sea salt and ground white pepper,
   to taste

2 tablespoons fresh tarragon or
   sage leaves, chopped

Sour cream, to serve

100g (3½oz) smoked salmon, cut
   into thin strips, to serve

Preheat pressure cooker to medium heat or use sauté setting.

Add olive oil, butter and onion. Sauté until fragrant.

Add asparagus and sauté for 1 minute. Add diced potato and stock and bring to a slow simmer. Lock the lid in place.

Stovetop: Apply medium to high heat to achieve the seal and allow pressure to build up. Once high pressure is reached, turn to low heat and cook for 6 minutes.

Electric: Turn to medium pressure and cook for 6 minutes.

Use the quick release water method or quick release lever to release the pressure.

Add spinach leaves, seasoning and herbs. Simmer for another 2 minutes. Remove from the heat and blend with a stick blender until smooth.

Serve with a dollop of sour cream and a few strips of smoked salmon.

SPLIT PEA AND HAM SOUP

Preparation time: 5 minutes
Pressure cooking time: 20 minutes
Pressure release: Natural release method

4L (8 pints) vegetable stock
  (see page 25)
4 shallots, chopped
1 ham hock, skin removed
8 stems fresh thyme
2 bay leaves
400g (14oz) split peas
1 bunch fresh chives, chopped or
  4 spring onions, chopped
Pinch ground white pepper

Simmer vegetable stock in the pressure cooker.

Add shallots, ham hock and herbs. Simmer for 5 minutes and sprinkle split peas on top. Don't stir the peas as they will sink and scorch on the bottom. Lock the lid in place.

Stovetop: Apply medium to high heat to achieve the seal and allow pressure to build up. Once high pressure is reached, turn to low heat and cook for 20 minutes.

Electric: Turn to medium pressure and cook for 20 minutes.

Use the natural release method to release the pressure.

Carefully remove the ham hock and allow to rest. Shred the meat off the bone. Add the ham meat to the soup. Stir in chopped chives and white pepper, to taste.

Take care not to overseason this soup.

Like red wine, it gets better with age over the next few days.

CHICKEN NOODLE SOUP

Preparation time:	10 minutes
Pressure cooking time:	12 minutes
Pressure release:	Quick release water method

4 tablespoons olive oil

2 brown onions, chopped

4 stalks celery, chopped

2 carrots, chopped

8 brown mushrooms, sliced

4L (8 pints) chicken or vegetable
stock (see pages 24–25)

500g (1lb) whole chicken thigh,
bone in

6 stems fresh thyme leaves
(or 1 teaspoon dried)

2 bay leaves

6 parsley stems, leaves removed
and set aside for garnish

½ teaspoon cracked
black peppercorns

250g (8oz) spinach ravioli

Sea salt and white pepper, to taste

Preheat pressure cooker on medium heat or use sauté setting.

Add oil and sauté prepared vegetables for 4 minutes. Deglaze with stock and allow to simmer briefly. Add chicken, herbs and peppercorns. Lock the lid in place.

Stovetop: Apply medium to high heat to achieve the seal and allow pressure to build up. Once high pressure is reached, turn to low heat and cook for 12 minutes.

Electric: Turn to medium pressure and cook for 12 minutes.

Use the quick release water method or quick release lever to release the pressure.

Add ravioli and reserved parsley leaves. Simmer on low heat for 10 minutes.

Season with sea salt and white pepper to taste.

MINESTRONE AND CHORIZO SOUP

Preparation time:	20 minutes
Pressure cooking time:	20 minutes
Pressure release:	Quick release water method

3 tablespoons extra virgin olive oil

2 brown onions, finely chopped

1 chorizo sausage, chopped

2 cloves garlic, crushed

½ red capsicum (pepper),
   finely chopped

½ green capsicum (pepper),
   finely chopped

2 celery stalks, finely chopped

3L (6 pints) vegetable stock
   (see page 25)

2 small pieces smoked bacon bone

500g (1lb) borlotti or kidney
   beans, cooked

750ml (1½ pints) tomato
   pasta sauce

1 bay leaf

Sprigs of oregano and thyme

½ cabbage, finely chopped

1 zucchini (courgette), cubed

100g (3½oz) green beans, cut into
   1cm (½in) pieces

Grated Parmesan cheese, to garnish

Garlic bread, toasted, to serve

Preheat pressure cooker on medium heat or use sauté setting.

Heat olive oil and sauté brown onion, sausage and garlic until fragrant. Sauté vegetables for 3 minutes.

Deglaze with stock. Add bacon bones and all other ingredients, except for the cheese. Lock the lid in place.

Stovetop: Apply medium to high heat to achieve the seal and allow pressure to build up. Once high pressure is reached, turn to low heat and cook for 20 minutes.

Electric: Turn to medium pressure and cook for 20 minutes.

Use the quick release water method or quick release lever to release the pressure.

Adjust seasoning if required. Serve with grated Parmesan cheese and toasted garlic bread.

LEEK AND POTATO SOUP WITH GREEN LENTILS

Preparation time:	20 minutes
Pressure cooking time:	10 minutes
Pressure release:	Natural release method

6 medium-sized leeks, finely
   chopped (use the white part only)
4 stalks celery, finely chopped
4 tablespoons olive oil
6 large royal blue potatoes,
   unpeeled, cut into 1cm
   (½in) pieces
2L (4 pints) vegetable stock
   (see page 25)
2 bay leaves
Sea salt and white ground pepper,
   to taste
½ teaspoon ground nutmeg
1 x 400g (14oz) tin drained
   green lentils
½ cup (125g, 4oz) flat-leaf parsley,
   chopped

Preheat pressure on low heat or use sauté setting.

Gently sauté leeks and celery in olive oil until soft and translucent. Add potatoes, stock and bay leaves. Bring to a slow simmer. Lock the lid in place.

Stovetop: Apply medium to high heat to achieve the seal and allow pressure to build up. Once low pressure is reached, turn to low heat and cook for 10 minutes.

Electric: Turn to medium pressure and cook for 10 minutes.

Use the natural release method to release the pressure.

Season with salt, pepper and nutmeg to taste. Use a stick blender to puree the soup in pulses. Avoid overblending as the potato will go gummy.

While the soup is still warm, stir in the green lentils and parsley.

Adjust seasoning if required.

n fresh napoli

eese mustard

nade hot chill

chutney meat

n spice blend

n curry blend

SAUCES
AND
SPICES

GARDEN FRESH NAPOLI SAUCE

Preparation time: 15 minutes
Pressure cooking time: 30 minutes
Pressure release: Quick release water method

¼ cup (60ml, 2fl oz) extra virgin
    olive oil
1 large brown onion, finely chopped
6 cloves of garlic, peeled
    and crushed
½ seeded red chilli, chopped
4 tablespoons concentrated
    tomato paste
2kg (4lb) sweet ripened
    Roma tomato, peeled and
    roughly chopped *
6 stalks fresh oregano, or
    2 tablespoons dried oregano
3 bay leaves

SEASONING
3 tablespoons balsamic vinegar
1 tablespoon sugar
Sea salt and white ground pepper,
    to taste
1 cup (250g, 8oz) fresh basil
    leaves, chopped

Preheat pressure cooker on medium heat or use sauté setting.
    Add olive oil and slowly caramelise onion for
4 to 5 minutes.
    Add crushed garlic and chilli and sauté briefly until
fragrant. Add tomato paste, chopped tomato, oregano and
bay leaves. Lock the lid in place.
    Stovetop: Apply medium to high heat to achieve the
seal and allow pressure to build up. Once high pressure is
reached, turn to low heat and cook for 30 minutes.
    Electric: Turn to low pressure and cook for 30 minutes.
    Use the quick release water method or quick release lever
to release the pressure.
    Slowly simmer sauce for 10 to 15 minutes. Season
sauce with vinegar, sugar, salt, pepper and fresh chopped
basil leaves.

* If tomatoes aren't in season, substitute with 4 x 720ml
(1 ½ pint) jars tomato puree.

BASIC CHEESE
AND MUSTARD SAUCE

Preparation time: 10 minutes
Cooking time: 10 minutes

80g (2¾oz) butter
4 tablespoons plain
  (all-purpose) flour
3 cups (720ml, 1½ pints)
  warm milk
250g (8oz) Swiss or Gruyere
  cheese, grated
2 tablespoons seeded
  grain mustard
Sea salt and white pepper, to taste

Slowly melt the butter in a saucepan. Stir in flour and cook for 3 minutes on low heat.

Gradually whisk in the warm milk and bring to a boil, stirring constantly.

Whisk in the cheese and mustard, season to taste.

TAPENADE

Preparation time: 5 minutes

200g (7oz) pitted Kalamata olives *
4 anchovy fillets
1 tablespoon capers
3 cloves garlic, toasted
3 tablespoons unsalted cashews
¼ cup (60ml, 2fl oz) extra virgin
    olive oil, plus extra

Place olives, anchovies, capers, toasted garlic and cashews in the food processer and process until finely minced to a smooth paste.

With the motor still running, gradually add oil in a thin stream until well combined and a smooth paste forms.

* You can substitute the Kalamata with stuffed Queen of Spain green olives.

HOT! CHILLI TOMATO CHUTNEY

Preparation time: 10 minutes
Pressure cooking time: 6 minutes
Pressure release: Natural release method

2 medium brown onions,
   roughly chopped
¼ cup (60ml, 2fl oz) olive oil
100g (3½oz) red chilli, chopped
2 tablespoons seeded
   grain mustard
750ml (1½ pints) tomato
   pasta sauce
1 tablespoon mixed spice
200g (7oz) dark brown sugar
200ml (7fl oz) white balsamic
   vinegar or red wine vinegar
1 cup (250g, 8oz) mixed
   dried fruit

In a saucepan, slowly sweat onions in olive oil without browning. Add the chillies and cook for another 3 minutes on medium heat.

Add mustard, sauce, spice, sugar, vinegar and mixed fruit. Slowly simmer the chutney, covered, for 2 hours. Stir occasionally.

Use sterilised preserving jars with new seals.

Boil the glass jar and lid for 4 minutes. Use a set of clean tongs to retrieve the jars. Place them upside down to drain any water.

Use protective gloves and a clean ladle to fill the jars with chutney. Gently tap the full jars to remove trapped air. Attach the rubber seal and secure the lid.

Place a stainless steel steaming tray on the bottom of the pressure cooker. Add 2L (4 pints) water and bring to a boil. Place the sealed jars side by side on the steaming tray. Lock the lid in place.

Stovetop: Apply medium to high heat to achieve the seal and allow pressure to build up. Once high pressure is reached, turn to low heat and cook for 6 minutes.

Electric: Turn to medium pressure and cook for 6 minutes.

Use the natural release method or quick release lever to release the pressure.

Remove the jars. Check the seal, label and store in the pantry.

MEAT AND CHICKEN SPICE BLEND

3 tablespoons red crushed mustard
2 tablespoons whole fennel seeds
2 tablespoons ground fennel
2 teaspoons ground black pepper
2 teaspoons garlic powder
1 teaspoon chilli powder
2 teaspoons sea salt

Combine all the ingredients in a mixing bowl; mix well.

Use this blend as a rub, especially on meat and chicken before pressure cooking.

MOROCCAN AND CURRY BLEND 'RAS EL HANOUT'

2 tablespoons ground
  turmeric powder
2 teaspoons ground cardamom
1 tablespoon ground cinnamon
1 tablespoon ground chilli powder
2 teaspoons ground allspice
2 tablespoons ground cumin seeds
2 teaspoons ground
  coriander seeds
1 teaspoon ground nutmeg
1 teaspoon ground white pepper

Combine and blend well.

Store in a spice jar or tin with a rubber seal. It may be stored for up to six months.

on asparagus
room spinach
cotta basmat
uinoa jasmine
peas carrots
almonds pesto

RICES
AND
GRAINS

LEMON RISOTTO WITH ASPARAGUS

Preparation time:	15 minutes
Pressure cooking time:	4 minutes
Pressure release:	Natural release method
Resting time:	15 to 20 minutes

50g (1¾oz) butter, plus
    100g (3½oz) extra
1 brown onion, finely chopped
2 cups (500g, 1lb) Arborio
    rice, washed
175ml (6fl oz) white wine
1½ L (3 pints) chicken or
    vegetable stock (see Stocks and
    Soups), simmering
Sea salt and white pepper, to taste
100g (3½oz) asparagus, sliced
100g (3½oz) pecorino
    cheese, grated
½ cup (125g, 4oz) flat-leaf
    parsley, chopped
¼ cup (60g, 2oz) dill, chopped
Zest and juice of 1 lemon

Preheat pressure cooker on medium heat or use sauté setting.

Add 50g (1¾oz) butter and onion and sauté until soft and transparent. Stir through rice and coat well with the cooked onion.

Deglaze with wine. Add hot simmering stock to the rice, stir, and allow the rice and stock to simmer briefly. Lock the lid in place.

Stovetop: Apply medium to high heat to achieve the seal and allow pressure to build up. Once high pressure is reached, turn to low heat and cook for exactly 4 minutes.

Electric: Turn to high pressure and cook for exactly 4 minutes.

Remove pressure cooker from heat. Use the natural release method to finish cooking the risotto.

Season with 100g (3½oz) butter, salt and pepper. Add asparagus, cheese, herbs, lemon zest and juice.

Rest the risotto for another 4 minutes before serving.

A great idea for this dish is to add some fresh scallops, sautéed for 30 seconds, or toss in 250g (8oz) shredded cooked crab or lobster meat.

BASMATI RICE AND RED QUINOA

Preparation time:	15 minutes
Pressure cooking time:	4 minutes
Pressure release:	Natural release method

4 tablespoons olive oil
2 cups (500g, 1lb) unwashed
  Basmati rice
3 cups (1 ½ pints) vegetable stock
  (see Stocks and Soups)
1 cup (250g, 8oz) red or
  white quinoa
½ cup (125g, 4oz) coriander
  leaves, chopped
Sea salt and pepper, to taste

Preheat pressure cooker on low heat or use sauté setting.

Add olive oil and Basmati rice. Gently sauté rice until fragrant, about 3 minutes. Stir in stock and quinoa and bring to a gentle boil. Lock the lid in place.

Stovetop: Apply medium to high heat to achieve the seal and allow pressure to build up. Once high pressure is reached, turn to low heat and cook for 4 minutes.

Electric: Turn to high pressure and cook for exactly 4 minutes.

Remove pressure cooker from the heat. Use the natural release method to release the pressure.

Season with coriander leaves, salt and pepper.

MUSHROOM, SPINACH AND BAKED RICOTTA RISOTTO

Preparation time:	20 minutes
Pressure cooking time:	4 minutes
Resting time:	20 minutes
Pressure release:	Natural release method

1 brown onion, finely chopped

4 tablespoons extra virgin olive oil

200g (7oz) mixed
mushrooms, sliced

3 cloves garlic, crushed

1 cup (250g, 8oz) Arborio rice
(washed through)

¼ cup (60ml, 2fl oz) verjuice
(unfermented white wine)

1L (2 pints) vegetable stock (see
Stocks and Soups), simmering

Sea salt and white pepper, to taste

½ cup (125g, 4oz) basil leaves,
finely chopped

1 cup (250g, 8oz) sweet fresh
corn kernels

100g (3½oz) baked ricotta
cheese, diced

125g (4oz) spinach leaves,
chopped, sautéed and squeezed

Pecorino shavings, to serve

Preheat pressure cooker on medium heat or use sauté setting.

Add onion and olive oil. Cook out onion until fragrant and lightly coloured. Add sliced mushrooms and sauté for 3 minutes or until fragrant. Add garlic and stir.

Stir in rice and coat well. Deglaze with verjuice or wine and stir through. Add simmering stock. Stir rice until it is well coated with the stock. Lock the lid in place.

Stovetop: Apply medium to high heat to achieve the seal and allow pressure to build up. Once high pressure is reached, turn to low heat and cook for 4 minutes.

Electric: Turn to high pressure and cook for exactly 4 minutes.

Use the natural release method to release the pressure.

Add seasoning, basil, corn, cheese and spinach. Serve with pecorino cheese shavings.

JASMINE YELLOW RICE WITH PEAS, CARROTS AND TOASTED ALMONDS

Preparation time:	5 minutes
Pressure cooking time:	6 minutes
Pressure release:	Natural release method

3 tablespoons olive oil

50g (1¾oz) butter

2 cups (500g, 1lb) Jasmine rice,
    washed through a sieve

1 teaspoon turmeric, ground

2 cups (500ml, 1 pint) vegetable
    stock (see Stocks and Soups)
    or water

1 cup (250g, 8oz) carrots, grated

1 cup (250g, 8oz) frozen peas

½ cup (125g, 4oz)
    parsley, chopped

½ cup (125g, 4oz) flaked
    almonds, toasted

Preheat pressure cooker on medium heat or use sauté setting.

Add oil, butter, rice and turmeric and sauté for 2 minutes. Add stock and bring to a rapid boil, giving a final stir. Lock the lid in place.

Stovetop: Apply medium to high heat to achieve the seal and allow pressure to build up. Once high pressure is reached, turn to low heat and cook for 6 minutes.

Electric: Turn to high pressure and cook for exactly 6 minutes.

Remove from heat and allow to sit for 15 minutes until the rice is fully cooked.

Stir through carrots, peas, chopped parsley and almonds.

This dish is excellent served with curries, barbequed seafood and meat.

PESTO RISOTTO WITH PEAS

Preparation time:	10 minutes
Pressure cooking time:	6 minutes
Pressure release:	Natural release method

3 tablespoons olive oil

1 brown onion, finely chopped

3 cloves garlic, crushed

1L (2 pints) chicken or vegetable
  stock (see Stocks and Soups)

1 cup (250g, 8oz) Arborio
  rice, washed

200g (7oz) fresh or frozen peas

100g (7oz) Pecorino
  cheese, grated

3 tablespoons pesto

Sea salt and white pepper, to taste

½ cup (125g, 4oz) flat-leaf
  parsley, chopped

50g (1¾oz) butter, optional

Preheat pressure cooker on medium heat or use sauté setting.

Add olive oil, onion and garlic. Gently sauté until fragrant. Add stock and bring to a slow boil. Stir in washed rice until it is well coated with the stock. Lock the lid in place.

Stovetop: Apply medium to high heat to achieve the seal and allow pressure to build up. Once high pressure is reached, turn to low heat and cook for 6 minutes.

Electric: Turn to high pressure and cook for exactly 6 minutes.

Use the natural release method to release the pressure.

Stir through peas, cheese, pesto, seasoning, parsley and butter (if desired). Rest the risotto for another 3 minutes before serving.

ansak chicken
y spinach red
entils eggplant
flower curried
nanks chicken
prawn laksa

CURRIES

DHANSAK CHICKEN CURRY WITH SPINACH AND RED LENTILS

Preparation time:	25 minutes
Pressure cooking time:	10 minutes
Pressure release:	Quick release water method

1 large red onion, thinly sliced

3 tablespoons extra virgin olive oil

3 tablespoons Moroccan and curry blend (see Sauces and Spices)

1 x 750g (1½lb) jar roast garlic and tomato pasta sauce

1 cup (250ml, 8fl oz) chicken stock (see Stocks and Soups)

8 chicken thighs, bone in

100g (3½oz) red lentils

100g (3½oz) fresh spinach, chopped

½ cup (125g, 4oz) coriander leaves

¼ cup (60g, 2oz) fresh mint

Salt and pepper, to taste

Preheat pressure cooker on medium heat or use sauté setting.

Brown onion in olive oil for 10 minutes or until well caramelised.

Add Moroccan and curry blend and cook for 2 to 3 minutes, or until fragrant. Stir in pasta sauce and chicken stock and bring to a slow boil.

Scatter chicken thighs on the sauce. Bring to a slow boil and sprinkle lentils over chicken (don't stir in lentils).

Stovetop: Lock lid at low pressure and cook for 10 minutes.

Electric: Turn to low pressure and cook for 10 minutes.

Release pressure using the quick release water method or quick release lever.

Toss in spinach leaves, coriander and mint leaves. Season to taste.

Serve with a steaming bowl of basmati rice and red quinoa (see Rices and Grains).

EGGPLANT AND CAULIFLOWER CURRY

Preparation time:	15 minutes
Pressure cooking time:	6 minutes
Pressure release:	Quick release water method

2 onions, sliced

3 tablespoons olive oil

2 tablespoons Moroccan and curry
  blend (see Sauces and Spices)

2 carrots, diced

1 whole cauliflower, cut into florets

8 baby eggplants (aubergines), cut
  in 2cm (1in) thick slices

2 x 250g (8oz) punnets crushed
  mini tomatoes or 2 tins whole
  peeled tomato

200g (7oz) mushrooms, sliced

2 cups (500ml, 1 pint) vegetable
  stock (see Stocks and Soups)

1 cup (250ml, 8fl oz)
  coconut cream

1 bunch pak-choy, cut into thirds

1 cup (250g, 8oz) coriander
  leaves, chopped

½ cup (125g, 4oz)
  almonds, crushed

Salt and pepper, to taste

Fine rice noodles, to serve

Preheat pressure cooker on low heat or use sauté setting.

Caramelise onions in olive oil. Add spice blend and sauté until fragrant.

Toss in carrots, cauliflower, eggplants, tomatoes, mushrooms and vegetable stock.

Stovetop: Lock lid at low pressure and cook for 6 minutes.

Electric: Turn to low pressure and cook for 6 minutes.

Release pressure using the quick release water method or quick release lever.

Add coconut cream and pak-choy. Cook for 5 minutes, then season with coriander, almonds, salt and pepper.

Serve with fine rice noodles.

CURRIED LAMB SHANKS

Preparation time:	25 minutes
Pressure cooking time:	30 minutes
Pressure release:	Quick release water method

6 French cut lamb shanks,
   dusted in flour, salt and white
   ground pepper
4 tablespoons olive oil
3 red onions, finely sliced
6 cloves garlic, crushed
3 tablespoons Moroccan and Curry
   blend (see Sauces and Spices)
2L (4 pints) beef, chicken or
   vegetable stock (see Stocks
   and Soups)
1 cup (250ml, 8fl oz) tomato
   pasta sauce
¼ cup (60ml, 2fl oz) white
   wine vinegar
3 tablespoons tomato chutney
½ cup (125g, 4oz) whole
   coriander, roots, stems and
   leaves, chopped
¼ cup (60g, 2oz) dill, chopped
Sea salt and white pepper

Preheat pressure cooker on medium heat or use sauté setting.

Brown lamb shanks in olive oil, a few at a time. Add onions and garlic and slowly cook until fragrant. Add spice blend and cook for 2 minutes, or until fragrant.

Deglaze with stock, tomato sauce and vinegar. Bring to a slow simmer. Return lamb shanks to the cooking liquid and return to a simmer. Lock the lid in place.

Stovetop: Apply medium to high heat to achieve the seal and allow pressure to build up. Once high pressure is reached, turn to low heat and cook for 30 minutes.

Electric: Turn to medium pressure and cook for 30 minutes.

Use the quick release water method or quick release lever to release the pressure.

Remove the shanks. Return liquid to a simmer. Add chutney, chopped herbs and season to taste.

Serve with basmati rice and red quinoa (see Rices and Grains).

CHICKEN AND PRAWN LAKSA

Preparation time:	20 minutes
Pressure cooking time:	7 minutes
Pressure release:	Quick release water method

4 heaped tablespoons laksa paste
  or red Thai chilli paste
3 tablespoons grapeseed oil
1 stem lemon grass, crushed
  and chopped
1 red chilli, chopped
1L (2 pints) chicken stock
  (see Stocks and Soups)
300g (10oz) free-range chicken
  thigh, thinly sliced
150g (5oz) prawns, deveined
1 x 400ml (13fl oz) tin
  coconut cream
Salt and pepper, to taste
½ brick vermicelli noodles, cooked
  to instructions and refreshed
60g (2oz) bean sprouts
Crisp fried shallots
2 green onions, thinly chopped
½ cup (60g, 2oz) coriander
  leaves, chopped

Preheat the pressure cooker on low to medium heat or use sauté setting.

Heat laksa paste with grapeseed oil until fragrant. Add lemon grass and chilli and cook until fragrant. Deglaze with chicken stock and stir the bottom to loosen the cooked paste. Toss in chicken and prawns. Lock the lid in place.

Stovetop: Apply medium to high heat to achieve the seal and allow pressure to build up. Once high pressure is reached, turn to low heat and cook for 7 minutes.

Electric: Turn to low pressure and cook for 7 minutes.

Use the quick release water method or quick release lever to release the pressure.

Pour in coconut cream and slowly simmer for 4 minutes. Season with salt and pepper to taste.

To serve, portion noodles into each bowl. Ladle laksa over the top. Garnish with sprouts, fried shallots, green onion slices and coriander leaves.

aligot mashed
tato steamed
ed vegetables
kipfler potato
ad cauliflower
chini steamed

VEGETABLES

PRESSURE COOKED VEGETABLES

TIME CHART

Artichoke (globe)..9 minutes on high pressure
Asparagus spears...2 minutes on high pressure
Beetroot ....20 minutes on high pressure
Broccoli stalks ....3 minutes on high pressure
Broccolini...2 minutes on high pressure
Brussells sprouts ....4 minutes on high pressure
Carrot sticks...4 minutes on high pressure
Cauliflower ....4 to 5 minutes on high pressure
Corn on the cob...3 minutes on high pressure
Frozen peas..2 minutes on high pressure
Green beans ....2 minutes on high pressure
Peas in the pod ....1 minute on low pressure
Potato, new, whole ....10 minutes on high pressure
Potato, large..12 to 15 minutes on high pressure
Snow peas..1 minute on low pressure
Sugar snaps ....1 minute on low pressure
Sweet potato, 30cm...6 minutes on high pressure
Zucchini (courgette), 25cm..................................3 minutes on high pressure

ALIGOT MASHED POTATO

Preparation time: 10 minutes
Pressure cooking time: 10 minutes
Pressure release: Quick release water method

500g (1lb) royal blue or ruby lou
   potatoes (skin on) cut into
   large cubes
4 cloves garlic, crushed
200g (7oz) Ambrosia or havarti
   cheese, grated
1 cup (250g, 8oz) flat-leaf
   parsley, chopped
2 tablespoons extra virgin olive oil
Sea salt and pepper, to taste

Place trivet in the pressure cooker and fill with enough water so it is just covered.

Place potato and garlic in the stainless steel steaming tray.

Stovetop: Lock lid and cook potatoes at high pressure for 10 minutes on low heat.

Electric: Turn to high pressure and cook for 10 minutes.

Use the quick release water method or quick release lever to release the pressure.

Remove potatoes. (Be careful, they are hot!) Empty out water and return the potatoes to the cooker. Crush steaming potato and garlic. Add cheese, parsley and oil. Season with salt and pepper.

Beat crushed potato with a wooden spoon until smooth and an elastic puree texture forms.

Set aside and keep warm to serve.

Excellent with a beef or chicken braise, or to top off a shepherd's pie.

THAI COLESLAW SALAD

Preparation time: 15 minutes

DRESSING
¼ cup (60ml, 2fl oz) fresh lime juice
¼ cup (60ml, 2fl oz) sweet
   Thai chilli sauce
2 tablespoons fish sauce

SALAD
1 Chinese cabbage, finely shredded
1 cucumber, seeded and
   finely chopped
½ red onion, finely shredded
2 red chilli, finely chopped
2 handfuls bean sprouts
1 carrot, grated
1 cup (250gm, 8oz) mint leaves

GARNISH
1 bunch chives, chopped
2 cups (500gm, 1lb)
   coriander leaves
½ cup (125gm, 4oz) cashew nuts,
   roasted and chopped

Whisk dressing ingredients together.
   Toss salad ingredients together with the dressing and add garnishes.

STEAMED MIXED VEGETABLES

Preparation time:	10 minutes
Pressure cooking time:	8 minutes
Pressure release:	Steaming mode, unlocked

500g (1lb) royal blue potatoes, cut
   into quarters
4 carrots, cut into large batons
½ cauliflower, cut into large florets
250g (8oz) stringless beans,
   tips removed
6 celery sticks, cut into quarters
200g (7oz) Swiss
   brown mushrooms
2 tablespoons extra virgin olive oil
Sea salt and pepper, to taste
½ cup (125g, 4oz) flat-leaf
   parsley, chopped

Fill the pressure cooker with 1L (2 pints) of water.

Place trivet and stainless steel steaming tray in the pressure cooker.

Bring water to a rapid boil. Cook potatoes in the perforated pan for 4 minutes with the lid unlocked (or on steaming mode).

Add the rest of the prepared vegetables and cook at low pressure for another 4 minutes.

Carefully remove steamed vegetables. Season with olive oil, salt, pepper and chopped parsley.

KIPFLER POTATO SALAD

Pressure cooking time: 6 to 8 minutes
Pressure release: Quick release water method

1kg (2lb) Kipfler potatoes,
  unpeeled, cut into 2cm pieces
2 bunches chives, chopped, or
  green spring onions
250g (8oz) crispy bacon
6 hard-boiled eggs
200g (7oz) cheddar cheese,
  cut into 1cm dice
250g (8oz) roasted capsicum
  (pepper) strips
3 handfuls rocket or watercress
  leaves, roughly chopped
1 cup (250g, 8oz) flat-leaf
  parsley, chopped

DRESSING
½ cup (125g, 4oz) piccalilli, tomato
  relish or any chutney
  with a bite
½ cup (125ml, 4fl oz) mayonnaise
3 tablespoons sour cream

Toasted pine nuts, to garnish

Place potatoes in the pressure cooker.

Stovetop: Pressure cook potatoes in 2L (4 pints) of water on low heat for 8 minutes or until tender but firm.

Electric: Turn to high pressure and cook for 8 minutes.

Use the quick release water method or quick release lever to release excess pressure.

Refresh potatoes in cold water to stop the cooking process. Allow the potatoes to cool. Toss the rest of the ingredients together to form the salad.

To make the dressing, combine piccalilli, mayonnaise and sour cream.

Toss piccalilli dressing through the salad, garnish with pine nuts and serve.

CAULIFLOWER AND ZUCCHINI

Preparation time:	4 minutes
Pressure cooking time:	5 minutes
Pressure release:	Quick release water method

½ cauliflower, cut in large florets
1 large zucchini (courgette), cut in
   1.5cm (½in) rounds

Fill pressure cooker with enough water to just touch the steaming tray. Fill the steaming tray with prepared vegetables.

Stovetop: Bring the water to a slow boil. Lock in lid and turn to high pressure. Reduce the heat to low and cook vegetables for 5 minutes.

Electric: Turn to high pressure and cook for 5 minutes.

Release pressure using the quick release water method or quick release lever.

Remove the vegetables and serve.

STEAMED MIXED CABBAGE

Preparation time: 15 minutes
Pressure cooking time: 15 minutes, steaming mode, unlocked

3 red onions, finely chopped
4 tablespoons olive oil
½ red cabbage, thinly shredded
½ Chinese cabbage,
   thinly shredded
½ green cabbage, thinly shredded
¼ cup white vinegar
1 tablespoon meat and chicken
   spice blend (see Sauces
   and Spices)
½ cup green onions, chopped
1 tablespoon brown sugar
Salt and pepper, to taste

Preheat pressure cooker on medium heat or use sauté setting.

Cook onion in the olive oil. Add shredded cabbage and stir until the cabbage is just starting to cook.

Attach lid to the pressure cooker but don't lock it. Leave on steaming setting for 4 minutes. Deglaze the cabbage with vinegar. Add spice blend, green onions and sugar. Season to taste.

Great with garlic chicken and a side of freshly cooked egg noodles.

NEW BABY POTATOES

Preparation time:	2 minutes
Pressure cooking time:	10 minutes
Pressure release:	Quick release water method

1kg (2lb) new baby potatoes
3 tablespoons Italian salad dressing
3 tablespoons chives, chopped
4 tablespoons sour cream

Fill pressure cooker with water to just under the steaming tray level. Place potatoes on the stainless steel steaming tray.

Stovetop: Lock in lid and cook potatoes at high pressure on low heat for 10 minutes.

Electric: Turn to high pressure and cook for 10 minutes.

Release pressure using the quick release water method or quick release lever.

Remove potato in the basket and place in a serving dish. Season potato with dressing, chives and sour cream.

SWEET POTATO PUREE

Preparation time:	10 minutes
Pressure cooking time:	6 minutes
Pressure release:	Quick release water method

1.5kg (3lb) sweet potatoes, peeled
  and roughly cut
3 tablespoons butter
2 tablespoons sea salt
1 teaspoon white pepper
2 tablespoons brown sugar
2 tablespoons lemon juice
Pinch ground nutmeg
Pinch ground cinnamon
½ cup (125g, 4oz) sage leaves,
  finely chopped

Place trivet and stainless steel steaming tray on the bottom of the pressure cooker. Place the prepared sweet potatoes in the steaming tray.

Fill pressure cooker with 2L (4 pints) water. Bring water to the boil. Lock the lid in place.

Stovetop: Apply medium to high heat to achieve the seal and allow pressure to build up. Once high pressure is reached, turn to low heat and cook for 6 minutes.

Electric: Turn to high pressure and cook for 6 minutes.

Use the quick release water method or quick release lever to release the pressure.

Remove the cooked sweet potato and place in a saucepan. Mash with a potato masher and add the remaining ingredients. Adjust seasoning if required.

RED QUINOA AND PUMPKIN SALAD

Preparation time: 20 minutes

1 cup (250g, 8oz) red quinoa

DRESSING
⅓ cup (100ml, 2¾fl oz) extra
    virgin olive oil
4 tablespoons lemon juice

SALAD
10 red radishes, sliced into rings
1 red onion, finely diced
2 punnets grape tomatoes, cut in half
150g (5oz) barbequed or roasted
    red capsicum
3 big handfuls rocket leaves
2 cups (500g, 1lb) chopped
    Italian parsley
150g (5oz) grated raw
    Japanese pumpkin
⅓ cup (100g, 3½oz)
    drained capers
¾ cup (180g, 6oz) Danish
    fetta, crumbled

Bring 2 cups (500ml, 1 pint) water to the boil in a saucepan.
Add quinoa, put on lid and slowly boil for 5 minutes. Remove
from heat and allow the quinoa to absorb water for another
10 minutes. Allow to cool down.

   To make the dressing, whisk olive oil through the
lemon juice.

   Toss in salad ingredients and garnish with crumbled
Danish fetta.

risotto green

gorgonzola

bean tapas

braised squid

ussels verjuice

marinated fish

SEAFOOD

SEAFOOD RISOTTO WITH GREEN PEAS AND DOLCE GORGONZOLA

Preparation time:	10 minutes
Pressure cooking time:	4 minutes
Pressure release:	Natural release method

50g (1½oz) butter

1 brown onion, finely chopped

2 cups (500g, 1lb) Arborio
  rice, washed

175ml (6fl oz) white wine

1½L (3 pints) seafood,
  chicken or vegetable stock
  (see Stocks and Soups), simmering

100g (3oz) butter, extra

Sea salt and white pepper, to taste

100g (3oz) Gorgonzola pieces

½ cup (125g, 4oz) thawed
  green peas

½ cup (125g, 4oz) flat-leaf parsley,
  chopped

¼ cup (60g, 2oz) dill, chopped

400g (14oz) mixed seafood:
  prawns, mussels and white fish
  fillet chunks

3 tablespoons olive oil

Preheat pressure cooker on medium heat or use sauté setting.

Add 50g (1½oz) butter and onions and sauté until soft and transparent. Stir through rice and coat well with the cooked onion. Deglaze with wine. Add hot simmering stock to the rice, stir, and allow the rice and stock to simmer briefly. Lock the lid in place.

Apply medium to high heat to achieve the seal and allow pressure to build up. Once high pressure is reached, turn to low heat and cook for exactly 4 minutes.

Electric: Turn to low pressure and cook for 4 minutes.

Remove pressure cooker from heat. Use the natural release method to finish cooking the risotto.

Season with 100g (3½oz) butter, salt and pepper. Add cheese, peas and herbs.

Sauté seafood in olive oil. Add to risotto and rest for 4 minutes before serving.

OCTOPUS AND BEAN TAPAS SALAD

Preparation time:	10 minutes
Pressure cooking time:	6 minutes
Pressure release:	Quick release water method

1 – 1.5kg (2 – 3lb) frozen octopus,
 slowly thawed
100ml (3½fl oz) white vinegar
2 bay leaves
9 whole peppercorns
1 red dried chilli
3 tablespoons olive oil
6 tablespoons extra virgin olive oil
2 tablespoons white
 balsamic vinegar
100g (3½oz) stringless runner
 beans, trimmed
100g (3½oz) borlotti beans
100g (3½oz) sugar snaps
125g (4oz) snow pea shoots
50g (1½oz) tapenade
 (see Sauces and Spices)
150g (5oz) Danish fetta
 cheese, crumbled
Toasted garlic bread, to serve

Prepare the octopus by cutting the tentacles 2cm (1in) from the tip. Pat dry with kitchen paper. Poke a few holes in the tentacles with a paring knife to allow excess pressure to be released while cooking.

Add 2L (4 pints) water, white vinegar, bay leaves, peppercorns, chilli and oil. Slowly bring to a boil. Add prepared octopus. Lock the lid on.

Stovetop: Apply medium to high heat to achieve the seal and allow pressure to build up. Once high pressure is reached, turn to low heat and cook for exactly 6 minutes.

Electric: Turn to low pressure and cook for 6 minutes.

Use the quick release water method or quick release lever and carefully remove the octopus. Refresh in a sink filled with iced water until cool.

Quickly blanch borlotti beans in salted boiling water for 3 minutes, then refresh. Drain and wash the beans.

Whisk extra virgin olive oil and balsamic vinegar until blended. Add drained beans, sugar snaps, snow pea shoots, tapenade, fetta and cooked octopus. Toss the salad until it is well combined.

Serve as tapas with some toasted garlic bread.

*Safety note: Meats of any sort build up pressure within the tissue, so be careful when removing the cooked octopus from the pressure cooker. Always use long tongs or a slotted cook's spoon.

BRAISED SQUID AND MUSSELS IN VERJUICE BROTH

Preparation time:	15 minutes
Pressure cooking time:	6 minutes
Pressure release:	Quick release water method

2 chopped red chillies

3 cloves garlic, crushed

3 tablespoons extra virgin olive oil

3 tablespoons tomato paste

A few thyme leaves

2 cups (500ml, 1 pint) white wine
   or verjuice

1 cup (250ml, 8fl oz) seafood
   stock or chicken stock (see Stocks
   and Soups)

250g (8oz) chopped Roma
   tomatoes, seeds removed

750g (1½lb) cleaned
   fresh mussels

250g (8oz) baby squid tubes
   or octopus

1 cup (250g, 8oz) flat-leaf
   parsley, chopped

Crusty bread, to serve

Greek salad, to serve

Preheat pressure cooker on medium heat or use sauté setting.

Sauté chillies and garlic in olive oil until fragrant. Add tomato paste and cook for 1 minute. Add thyme and deglaze with wine, scraping the bottom. Add stock and chopped tomatoes. Bring to a rolling boil. Stir in the seafood. Lock the lid on.

Stovetop: Apply medium to high heat to achieve the seal and allow pressure to build up. Once high pressure is reached, turn to low heat and cook for 6 minutes.

Electric: Turn to low pressure and cook for 6 minutes.

Use the quick release water method or quick release lever to release pressure. Remove seafood with a slotted spoon and set aside. Reduce sauce by one-third.

Serve the seafood separately, topped with chopped parsley. Place sauce on the side with lots of crusty bread and a fresh Greek salad.

MARINATED FISH WRAPPED IN NORI WITH SOY AND PINE NUT SAUCE

Preparation time:	20 minutes
Pressure cooking time:	4 minutes
Cooking pressure:	Unlocked low pressure or steam setting

500g (1lb) fresh fish fillet—pink
   snapper, red emperor or
   salmon steaks
2 tablespoons light soy sauce
Few drops sesame seed oil
2 tablespoons sweet chilli sauce
Toasted sesame seeds
1 packet seaweed nori
1 stem lemon grass
2cm (1in) piece of ginger
4 bok choys, split in half

DRESSING
1 teaspoon sesame seed oil
2 tablespoons light soy sauce
2 tablespoons rice vinegar
2 tablespoons roasted pine nuts,
   finely crushed

Pat fresh fish with kitchen towels to remove excess moisture. Combine soy, sesame seed oil and chilli sauce to make a simple marinade.

Coat the fish in the marinade and allow to rest for 5 minutes so the fish picks up the flavours.

Season flesh side of the fish with sesame seeds, then gently wrap in nori.

Fill with enough water to just touch the stainless steel steaming tray. Add lemon grass and ginger and simmer for 3 minutes to infuse the aromatics.

Place the prepared fish side by side on the stainless steel steaming tray.

Set the heat to high but don't lock the pressure cooker. Use the steaming setting if available.

Steam fish for 4 minutes, then carefully remove with tongs and oven mitts. Steam the bok choy for 2 minutes and serve with the fish.

To make the dressing, combine all ingredients and serve alongside the dish.

ted beet osso

co marinated

rk belly strips

rbequed pork

esy quesadilla

veal shoulde

MEATS

BASIC POT ROASTED BEEF

Preparation time: 15 minutes

Pressure cooking time: 35 to 40 minutes

Pressure release: Quick release water method

1.5kg (3lb) whole chuck roast, patted dry with kitchen paper

½ teaspoon ground white pepper

1 tablespoon sea salt

1 tablespoon smoked or sweet paprika

3 tablespoons olive oil

250g (8oz) ox tails

2 cups (500ml, 1 pint) beef or vegetable stock (see Stocks and Soups)

⅓ cup (70ml, 2½fl oz) Worcestershire sauce (or a nice drop of red wine)

10 cloves whole garlic, peeled

2 bay leaves

1 tablespoon whole peppercorns

Trim any excess fat from the meat.

Season the beef with pepper, salt and paprika. Rub the olive oil on to the beef.

Preheat pressure cooker on medium heat or use sauté setting. Brown off the meat on all sides, then set aside.

Brown ox tails for 4 minutes. Deglaze with stock, sauce and garlic. Bring to a slow boil. Return the meat to the pressure cooker. Add bay leaves and peppercorns. Lock the lid in place.

Stovetop: Apply medium to high heat to achieve the seal and allow pressure to build up. Once high pressure is reached, turn to low heat and cook for 35 to 40 minutes.

Electric: Turn to high pressure and cook for 15 to 20 minutes.

Use the quick release water method or quick release lever to release the pressure.

Remove and discard bones. Rest the beef. Reduce the sauce for 10 minutes.

Serve with steamed vegetables (see Vegetables).

If you want to thicken the sauce, use 3 tablespoons of gravy powder per litre (2 pints) of cooking liquid. Whisk 300ml (10fl oz) cooking liquid to 5 tablespoons of thickener. Add into the cooking liquid.

OSSO BUCCO

Preparation time: 20 minutes
Pressure cooking time: 35 minutes
Pressure release: Quick release water method

6 thickly sliced veal shanks,
   patted dry
Salt and pepper, to taste
Pinch of paprika
4 tablespoons extra virgin olive oil
2 brown onions, diced
6 cloves garlic, crushed
250ml (8fl oz) white wine
250ml (8fl oz) beef stock
   (see Stocks and Soups)
400ml (13½fl oz) good quality
   tomato pasta sauce
Juice of 1 lemon
3 bay leaves
½ bunch fresh thyme stems and
   leaves (or 2 tablespoons
   dried thyme)

GREMOLATA GARNISH
Zest 1 lemon
½ cup (125g, 4oz) flat-leaf
   parsley, chopped
2 cloves garlic, crushed

Polenta, to serve

Preheat pressure cooker on medium heat or use sauté setting.

Season veal with salt, pepper and a pinch of paprika. Brown a few pieces at a time and set aside.

Add a splash of olive oil and slowly brown the onions and garlic. Deglaze with wine and stock. Scrape the bottom to remove the caramelised meat juices.

Evenly arrange the browned veal in the pressure cooker. Add pasta sauce, lemon juice and herbs. Lock the lid on.

Stovetop: Apply full heat to achieve the seal and pressure build up. Once at high pressure turn to very low heat and cook for 35 minutes.

Electric: Turn to high pressure and cook for 35 minutes.

Release pressure using the quick release water method or quick release lever.

Remove cooked veal and set the sauce aside for 20 minutes. Quickly brown the veal in a heavy-based skillet.

To make gremolata, mix all ingredients together.

Serve on a steaming portion of polenta, garnished with gremolata.

MARINATED PORK BELLY STRIPS

Preparation time:	20 minutes
Marinating time:	2 hours
Pressure cooking time:	15 minutes
Pressure release:	Quick release water method

MARINADE
2 shallots, finely chopped
2cm (1in) piece fresh
  ginger, crushed
1 stem lemon grass, crushed
  and chopped
2 tablespoons sweet Thai
  chilli sauce
3 tablespoons dark soy sauce
1 tablespoon brown sugar
1 star anise

1kg (2lb) lean pork belly strips

To make the marinade, mix all ingredients together.

Marinate the pork belly for a minimum of 2 hours, preferably overnight.

Fill pressure cooker with enough water to just reach the trivet and steaming tray. Drain pork pieces and reserve the marinating juices. Reduce marinade by half.

Set the pork strips side by side on the steaming tray.

Stovetop: Bring the pressure cooker to the boil. Lock the lid on. When high pressure is reached, turn to low heat and cook for 15 minutes.

Electric: Turn to high pressure and cook for 15 minutes.

Use the quick release water method or quick release lever to release pressure. Remove pork.

To serve, grill or barbeque the pork for 3 minutes on each side, basting with reduced glaze sauce.

Chop into 4cm (1½in) pieces and scatter on a Thai coleslaw salad (see Vegetables).

BARBEQUED PORK AND CHEESY QUESADILLA WRAPS

Preparation time:	20 minutes
Pressure cooking time:	40 minutes
Pressure release:	Quick release water method

2 brown onions, roughly diced
3 tablespoons olive oil
500g (1lb) shoulder pork roast
Salt and white pepper, to taste
500ml (1 pint) beef stock
1/3 cup (70ml, 2½fl oz) low-salt soya sauce
1 star anise
1 bay leaf
250ml (8fl oz) barbeque sauce

CHEESY QUESADILLA WRAPS
300g (10oz) tasty cheddar cheese, grated
6 mountain breads (or any flat wrapping bread)
1 tomato, chopped
1 iceberg lettuce, shredded
250g (8oz) sour cream
Coriander leaves

Preheat pressure cooker to medium heat or use sauté setting.

Slowly brown onions in olive oil until fragrant. Season pork with salt and pepper. Add pork to the onions.

Add stock, soya sauce, star anise and bay leaf. Bring to a rapid boil. Lock the lid on.

Stovetop: Apply medium to full heat to achieve the seal and pressure build up. Once at high pressure turn to very low heat and cook for 40 minutes.

Electric: Turn to high pressure and cook for 20 minutes.

Use the quick release water method or quick release lever to release the pressure.

Remove the pork and allow to rest before shredding with a fork. Reduce the cooking juices in the pressure cooker by two-thirds. Add the barbeque sauce and shredded pork. Reduce to a thick consistency.

Add a handful of grated cheese to a non-stick pan. Allow the cheese to turn golden brown. Lay the flat bread on top. Flip the bread over to expose the golden brown cheese.

Fill with shredded pork, tomato, lettuce, sour cream and coriander leaves. Roll up into a wrap.

Serve with a simple tossed salad with fresh mango and avocado.

SHREDDED MEXICAN
SALSA BEEF WRAPS

Preparation time:	10 minutes
Pressure cooking time:	20 minutes
Pressure release:	Natural release method

1 teaspoon ground cumin

1 teaspoon paprika

1 teaspoon salt

2 x 500g (1lb) skirt steaks, patted
   dry with kitchen paper

4 tablespoons olive oil

1 red onion, finely chopped

3 cloves garlic, crushed

1½ cups (12fl oz) beef stock
   (see Stocks and Soups)

375g (13oz) mild tomato salsa

Sea salt and ground white pepper,
   to taste

6 mountain breads (or any flat
   wrapping bread)

1 iceberg lettuce, shredded

1 avocado, sliced

250g (8oz) sour cream

Preheat pressure cooker on medium heat or use sauté setting.

Rub the spices and salt into the skirt steak. Brown the meat for 3 minutes per side in olive oil. Remove and rest the meat.

Add the onion and garlic. Sauté until fragrant. Return the meat and deglaze with the stock and salsa. Lock the lid in place.

Apply medium to high heat to achieve the seal and allow pressure to build up. Once high pressure is reached, turn to low heat and cook for 20 minutes.

Electric: Turn to high pressure and cook for 20 minutes.

Use the natural release method to release the pressure. Remove the beef and allow to rest.

Reduce the sauce for 10 to 12 minutes. While the sauce reduces, use a carving fork to shred the meat. Return the meat to the sauce and reduce further. Season with sea salt and ground white pepper to taste.

Serve on flat bread with grated cheddar cheese, lettuce, avocado and sour cream.

CLASSIC BRAISED CORNED BEEF AND CABBAGE

Preparation time:	20 minutes
Pressure cooking time:	45 minutes
Pressure release	Quick release water method

1kg (2lb) piece corned beef or
   girello (Italian silverside)
3 tablespoons olive oil
3 brown onions, peeled then
   roughly cut
2 bay leaves
500ml (1 pint) beef stock or
   vegetable stock (see Stocks
   and Soups)

BRAISED CABBAGE AND POTATO
750g (1 ½lb) whole baby
   chat potatoes
1 whole Savoy cabbage,
   finely sliced
2 tablespoons whole
   seeded mustard
3 tablespoons fresh thyme
   leaves, chopped
½ cup (125ml, 4fl oz) white vinegar
½ teaspoon ground white pepper
½ cup (125g, 4oz) flat-leaf parsley,
   chopped

Preheat pressure cooker until warm or use sauté setting.

Rinse off corned beef in cold, fresh water, pat dry. Brown corned beef in a little olive oil.

Sauté onions and bay leaves for 3 minutes or until fragrant. Deglaze with 500ml (1 pint) water and stock. Allow the stock to simmer. Lock the lid in place.

Stovetop: Apply medium to high heat to achieve the seal and allow pressure to build up. Once high pressure is reached, turn to low heat and cook for 45 minutes.

Electric: Turn to high pressure and cook for 20 minutes.

Use the quick release water method or quick release lever to release the pressure.

While the stock is simmering, stir in potatoes, cabbage, mustard, thyme and vinegar.

Stovetop: Attach the lid and set temperature to high until at high pressure. Turn to low heat and cook a further 4 minutes.

Electric: Turn to high pressure and cook for 4 minutes.

Use the quick release water method to release the pressure. Season with ground white pepper and parsley.

STUFFED TURKEY BREAST WITH TRUFFLE OIL, ONION, SAGE AND PINE NUTS

Preparation time:	25 minutes
Pressure cooking time:	30 to 35 minutes
Pressure release:	Quick release water method

1 white onion, finely chopped

3 tablespoons extra virgin olive oil

1 cup (250g, 8oz) minced fresh
   wholemeal bread

250g (8oz) pork sausage meat

1 egg

½ cup (125g, 4oz) sage
   leaves, chopped

50g (1½oz) pine nuts, toasted

1 tablespoon truffle oil or toasted
   sesame seed oil

½ cup (125g, 4oz) sour cream

2.6kg (6lb) turkey breast, butterflied
   by the butcher

Salt and pepper, to taste

TURKEY STOCK

1 onion, cut in quarters

2 carrots, cut in half

Celery heart

TURKEY GRAVY

5 tablespoons gravy powder

Sauté onion in olive oil until well caramelised. Add this to the breadcrumbs, pork mince, egg, sage, pine nuts, truffle oil and sour cream. Blend to a soft stuffing mixture.

Season the inside of the turkey with salt and pepper. Fill the centre with stuffing and roll up tightly with baking paper and aluminium foil.

If possible, allow the roll to rest in the refrigerator for 12 hours.

Fill pressure cooker with enough water to just touch the trivet and steaming tray. Add onion, carrots and celery to make a stock. Bring the stock to a rapid boil and lay the prepared turkey on the steaming tray. Lock the lid in place.

Stovetop: Apply medium to high heat to achieve the seal and allow pressure to build up. Once high pressure is reached, turn to low heat and cook for 30 to 35 minutes.

Electric: Turn to medium pressure and cook for 20 minutes.

Use the quick release water method or quick release lever to release pressure. Rest turkey for 10 minutes before carving.

Put gravy powder in a small saucepan. Whisk in 200ml (7fl oz) of cooking liquid to create a smooth paste. Add the rest of the stock and slowly simmer to a thick gravy consistency.

SEASONED TURKEY ROLL

Preparation time:	20 minutes
Pressure cooking time:	15 to 20 minutes
Pressure release:	Quick release water method
Resting time:	15 to 20 minutes before carving

2.2–2.7kg (5–6lb) turkey breast,
   patted dry with kitchen paper
2 cloves garlic, crushed
4 tablespoons extra virgin olive oil
Zest of 1 lemon
¼ cup (60g, 2oz) flat-leaf
   parsley, chopped
¼ cup (60g, 2oz) sage leaves
   or tarragon
1L (2 pints) chicken or vegetable
   stock (see Stocks and Soups)

GRAVY
4 tablespoons butter
4 tablespoons plain flour
3 tablespoons red currant
   conserve or jam
Sea salt and ground white pepper,
   to taste

Lift the skin off the turkey from the pointy end of the breast. Form a pocket between the skin and breast meat.

Sauté garlic in olive oil until fragrant but not coloured. Add zest and herbs and combine well. Fill the pocket under the skin with an even layer of seasoning.

Wrap the turkey in baking paper. Place the turkey in the steaming tray and set aside.

Fill the pressure cooker with stock and bring to a slow boil. Place steaming tray with turkey into the cooker and lock the lid in place.

Stovetop: Apply medium to high heat to achieve the seal and allow pressure to build up. Once high pressure is reached, turn to low heat and cook for 15 to 20 minutes.

Electric: Turn to medium pressure and cook for 10 to 15 minutes.

Use the quick release water method or quick release lever to release the pressure.

Remove and rest the cooked turkey, keeping wrapped until ready to serve. Reduce remaining stock.

In a separate saucepan, slowly cook butter and flour to make a roux. Mix in enough reduced stock to make a thick, textured sauce. Season gravy with jam, salt and pepper to taste.

Carve turkey roll into thick slices and serve with gravy.

VEAL SHOULDER
WITH MIXED MUSHROOMS

Preparation time:	20 minutes
Pressure cooking time:	25 minutes
Pressure release:	Quick release water method

1.5kg (3lb) lean veal shoulder meat,
   cut into 3–4cm (1–1½in) pieces
½ teaspoon ground white pepper
½ teaspoon paprika
½ teaspoon sea salt
4 tablespoons olive oil
6 cloves garlic, crushed
50g (1½oz) whole
   button mushrooms
50g (1½oz) shiitake mushrooms
100g (3½oz) large Portabello
   mushrooms, cut into quarters
1 cup (250ml, 8fl oz) dry
   white wine
3 cups (750ml, 1½ pints) beef
   or vegetable stock (see Stocks
   and Soups)
125g (4oz) fresh thyme leaves
1 tablespoon whole
   black peppercorns
4 tablespoons thickening agent,
   mixed through 300ml (10fl oz)
   cooking liquid

Preheat pressure cooker on medium heat or use sauté setting.

Season veal with pepper, paprika and sea salt.

Rub olive oil into the seasoned veal. Brown veal in small batches and set aside for later.

Add garlic and mushrooms. Sauté until the mushroom juices are reduced and fragrant.

Deglaze with wine and scrape the bottom to remove any caramelised veal juices. Add stock, herbs, peppercorns, browned veal and all the juices. Lock the lid in place.

Stovetop: Apply medium to high heat to achieve the seal and allow pressure to build up. Once high pressure is reached, turn to low heat and cook for 25 minutes.

Electric: Turn to high pressure and cook for 20 minutes.

Use the quick release water method or quick release lever to release the pressure.

Stir in thickening agent and simmer the veal on low heat for 3 minutes.

STRINGY SOY BEEF WITH BROCCOLINI

Preparation time:	30 minutes
Pressure cooking time:	35 to 40 minutes
Pressure release:	Quick release water method

2kg (4lb) whole skirt steak, patted
   dry with kitchen paper
Pinch of salt and pepper
2 tablespoons olive oil
1 onion, finely sliced
3 tablespoons extra virgin olive oil
2cm (1in) piece fresh ginger, crushed
3L (6 pints) beef or vegetable stock
   (see Stocks and Soups)
100ml (3½fl oz) low-salt soy sauce
1 cinnamon quill
1 star anise
¼ cup (60ml, 2fl oz) mirin
   or sweet wine
3 bunches broccolini

Preheat pressure cooker on medium heat or use sauté setting.

Season meat with salt and pepper. Rub in olive oil.

Brown beef until cooked and fragrant, turning once or twice. Remove browned meat to rest.

Sauté onion in extra virgin olive oil until fragrant. Add ginger, stock, soy sauce, cinnamon, star anise and mirin. Slowly bring to the boil. Place the meat on top of the stock. Lock the lid in place.

Stovetop: Apply medium to high heat to achieve the seal and allow pressure to build up. Once high pressure is reached, turn to low heat and cook for 35 to 40 minutes.

Electric: Turn to high pressure and cook for 20 minutes.

Release pressure using the quick release water method or quick release lever.

Strain off meat and reserve stock. Remove cinnamon and star anise. Reduce stock by one-third. Shred the beef with a fork while the sauce is reducing.

Preheat a large wok on medium heat. Add shredded beef to the wok and stir fry until the meat glazes. Add the reduced stock and broccolini. Stir fry briefly.

Serve on long grain rice (see Rices and Grains).

SUPER QUICK BOLOGNESE

Preparation time:	20 minutes
Pressure cooking time:	15 minutes
Pressure release:	Quick release water method

250g (8oz) ground beef mince
250g (8oz) ground pork mince
3 tablespoons extra virgin olive oil
3 cloves garlic, crushed
100ml (3½fl oz) beef or chicken
  stock (see Stocks and Soups)
2 tablespoons dried oregano
  or ½ bunch fresh oregano
2 x 700g (1½lb) jars pasta sauce
3 tablespoons extra virgin olive oil
Spaghetti, to serve
Parmesan cheese, to serve

Preheat pressure cooker to medium heat or use sauté setting.

Double brown mince in olive oil so there is no moisture left in the pot. Add garlic and cook until fragrant.

Deglaze with stock and scrape the bottom to remove and incorporate the juices. Stir in oregano, pasta sauce and extra virgin olive oil. Simmer. Lock the lid in place.

Stovetop: Apply medium to high heat to achieve the seal and allow pressure to build up. Once high pressure is reached, turn to low heat and cook for 15 minutes.

Electric: Turn to high pressure and cook for 15 minutes.

Use the quick release water method or quick release lever to release the pressure.

Season the sauce to taste and serve over steaming spaghetti noodles topped with Parmesan cheese.

butter chicken

garlic chicken

zo coq au vir

cken red wine

occan chicker

gine chickpeas

CHICKEN

BUTTER CHICKEN

Preparation time:	20 minutes
Marinating time:	12 hours
Pressure cooking time:	7 minutes
Pressure release:	Quick release water method

MARINADE
40g (1½oz) Moroccan and curry
blend (see Sauces and Spices)
1kg (2lb) chicken thigh meat, cut
into 4cm (2in) pieces
2cm (1in) piece ginger, crushed
4 garlic cloves, crushed
Juice of 1 lemon or lime
200g (7oz) Greek-style yoghurt

4 tablespoons olive oil
3 tablespoons olive oil, extra
2 medium brown onions,
finely chopped
2 cups (500ml, 1 pint) chicken or
vegetable stock (see Stocks and
Soups)
2 cups (500ml, 1 pint) tomato
puree or pasta sauce
2 bay leaves
3 coriander roots
1 cup (250ml, 8fl oz) full cream
1 tablespoon sugar
Salt and pepper, to taste
1 cup (250g, 8oz) coriander
leaves, roughly chopped

Rub the spice blend on to the chicken thigh meat until well coated. Add ginger, garlic, juice and yoghurt. Combine well and marinate, covered, for 12 hours in the fridge.

Preheat a large wok or frying pan on medium to high heat. Add olive oil and brown marinated chicken in small batches. Set aside.

Preheat pressure cooker to medium heat or use sauté setting. Add olive oil and caramelise onions until fragrant.

Add stock, tomato puree, herbs and browned chicken. Slowly simmer for 3 minutes. Lock the lid in place.

Stovetop: Apply medium to high heat to achieve the seal and allow pressure to build up. Once low pressure is reached, turn to low heat and cook for 7 minutes.

Electric: Turn to medium pressure and cook for 7 to 10 minutes.

Release pressure with the quick release water method or quick release lever.

Add cream, sugar and seasoning. Simmer for another 10 minutes before serving.

Serve on jasmine yellow rice with peas, carrots and toasted almonds (see Rices and Grains). Garnish with chopped coriander.

GARLIC CHICKEN AND CHORIZO

Preparation time: 15 minutes
Pressure cooking time: 12 minutes
Pressure release: Quick release water method

2 brown onions, cut into eighths
3 tablespoons extra virgin olive oil
20 cloves garlic, crushed
1 red chilli, finely chopped
500ml (1 pint) chicken stock (see
    Stocks and Soups)
500ml (1 pint) pasta
    sauce, simmered
250g (8oz) pitted Kalamata olives
¼ cup (60g, 2oz) chopped fresh or
    dried oregano leaves
2 whole chorizo sausages
1kg (2lb) chicken pieces
Salt and pepper, to taste
Polenta, to serve

Preheat pressure cooker on medium heat or use sauté setting.

Sauté onion in olive oil for 5 minutes until they just start to colour. Add garlic and chilli. Cook until fragrant.

Deglaze with stock and pasta sauce. Add olives and oregano leaves. Toss in chorizo and bring to the boil. Carefully place chicken pieces on the sauce. Lock the lid in place.

Stovetop: Apply medium to high heat to achieve the seal and allow pressure to build up. Once high pressure is reached, turn to low heat and cook for 12 minutes.

Electric: Turn to medium pressure and cook for 12 minutes.

Release the pressure with the quick release water method or quick release lever.

With a slotted spoon, remove the chicken pieces and set aside. Return the sauce to the heat. Simmer the sauce for another 10 minutes and season to taste.

Serve the chicken on soft polenta drizzled with sauce and sliced chorizo taken from the sauce.

MOROCCAN CHICKEN TAGINE WITH CHICKPEAS AND COUSCOUS

Preparation time:	20 minutes
Pressure cooking time:	10 minutes
Pressure release:	Quick release water method

4 tablespoons olive oil

2 medium brown onions

2 tablespoons Moroccan and curry
   blend (see Sauces and Spices)

1 small eggplant (aubergine),
   thickly sliced

2 cups (500ml, 1 pint) vegetable
   stock (see Stocks and Soups)

6 ripe whole tomatoes, sliced

2 tablespoons preserved
   lemons, chopped

2 cups (500g, 1lb) sweet
   potato, diced

1.5kg (3lb) chicken leg and thigh

2 x 400g (14oz) tins
   drained chickpeas

1 cinnamon quill

1 bay leaf

Sea salt and ground white pepper,
   to taste

Couscous, to serve

½ cup (125g, 4oz) mint
   leaves, chopped

½ cup (125g, 4oz) coriander
   leaves, chopped

Preheat pressure cooker on medium heat or use sauté setting.
   Add olive oil and sauté onion until fragrant.

   Add spice blend and sauté until fragrant, approximately 1 minute. Add eggplant, stock, tomatoes, preserved lemons and sweet potato. Bring to a slow simmer.

   Arrange the chicken pieces and chickpeas on top. Don't stir through. Add cinnamon and bay leaf, then simmer briefly. Lock the lid in place.

   Stovetop: Apply medium to high heat to achieve the seal and allow pressure to build up. Once high pressure is reached, turn to low heat and cook for 10 minutes.

   Electric: Turn to medium pressure and cook for 10 minutes.

   Use the quick release water method or quick release lever to release the pressure.

   Season with salt and pepper to taste.

   Serve on a steaming bowl of couscous with chopped fresh mint and coriander leaves.

COQ AU VIN
(CHICKEN IN RED WINE)

Preparation time:	20 minutes
Marinating time:	1 hour, ideally overnight
Pressure cooking time:	10 minutes
Pressure release:	Quick release water method

1 whole chicken, cut into
    8 large pieces
300ml (10fl oz) red wine (Shiraz)
3 cloves garlic, crushed
1 bay leaf
4 tablespoons olive oil
4 thick slices of smoked bacon,
    diced into pieces
100g (3½oz) peeled
    whole shallots
250g (8oz) button mushrooms
6 sprigs fresh thyme
6 stems parsley
3 bay leaves, extra
200ml (7fl oz) chicken stock
    (see Stocks and Soups)
375ml (¾ pint) red wine, extra
Freshly cracked pepper and sea
    salt, to taste

Marinate chicken pieces in red wine, garlic and bay leaf in a tight ziplock bag with most of the air pressed out.

Strain and reserve marinade.

Preheat pressure cooker on medium heat or use sauté setting.

Add olive oil, bacon, shallots and mushrooms. Sauté for 5 minutes. Add herbs and chicken stock. Simmer for 3 minutes. Add chicken pieces, reserved marinade and extra wine. Bring back to a slow simmer. Lock the lid in place.

Apply medium to high heat to achieve the seal and allow pressure to build up. Once high pressure is reached, turn to low heat and cook for 10 minutes.

Electric: Turn to medium pressure and cook for 10 minutes.

Use the quick release water method or quick release lever to release the pressure.

Remove chicken pieces and set aside. Return liquid to a simmer and reduce to a sauce consistency. Season with freshly cracked pepper and sea salt to taste.

Serve with steamed vegetables and aligot mashed potato (see Vegetables).

cot toffee best

lding carame

range poppy

eed christmas

t nut carame

rt sticky date

DESSERTS

PRESSURE COOKED DESSERT TIPS

If you think about it, a pressure cooker is just like an oven. You can use it to bake amazing puddings in no time. While steaming would take around 4 hours, a pressure cooker will have your dessert on the dinner table within 50 minutes.

Here are some useful tips for baking puddings in a pressure cooker. They use essentially the same procedure:

1. Insert a trivet on the bottom of the pressure cooker.
2. Fill with enough water to touch the trivet.
3. Use a stainless steel steaming tray on top of the trivet.
4. Line the pudding or soufflé dish with baking paper.
5. Rest the pudding or soufflé dish on the steaming tray.
6. Allow the completed pudding to rest in the tin for 5 minutes before cooking—this will allow the rising agents to become active and make the pudding spongier in texture.
7. All cooking times start when you get to high pressure; once at high pressure turn to low heat, and use a diffuser if you're using a gas ring.
8. Always use the quick release water method or quick release lever to release the pressure.
9. Most of the puddings in this book take around 45 to 50 minutes to cook.
10. Allow the pudding to cool down before serving.

DESSERT BASICS

SELF-RAISING FLOUR

4 cups (1kg, 2lb) plain (all-purpose) flour
2 teaspoons salt
4 tablespoons baking powder

Sift ingredients through a fine sieve 3 times.

It's good to make your own self-raising flour for pressure cooker puddings rather than using store-bought, as then you know it is fresh.

CARAMEL SAUCE

1 cup (250g, 8oz) brown sugar
150ml (5fl oz) cream
60g (2oz) butter

Quickly simmer sauce for 7 minutes, or until it becomes thick and creamy.

CHOC TOFFEE SAUCE

½ cup (125g, 4oz) brown sugar
1 cup (250ml, 8fl oz) cream
100g (3½oz) butter
100g (3½oz) dark chocolate pieces

Gently melt sugar, cream and butter to a rich sauce. Remove from the heat and allow to cool. Beat in chocolate pieces until smooth and rich.

RICH BUTTERSCOTCH SAUCE

1 cup (250ml, 8fl oz) cream
2 teaspoons vanilla essence
1 cup (250g, 8oz) dark brown sugar
200g (7oz) butter

Place the cream, vanilla, sugar and butter in a saucepan and slowly simmer for 5 to 7 minutes.

BRANDY CUSTARD SAUCE

4 egg yolks
60g (2oz) caster sugar
1 tablespoon custard powder
Pinch of salt
500ml (1 pint) slowly simmering milk
½ vanilla split pod
2 tablespoons brandy (or any liqueur)

Whisk egg yolks and sugar in a mixing bowl over a double boiler until thick and pale. Whisk in custard powder and a pinch of salt.

Slowly add simmering milk, infused with vanilla, 100ml (3½fl oz) at a time, whisking as you go. Repeat until all the milk has been incorporated.

Transfer to a lightly simmering double boiler and paddle back and forth with a beechwood spoon until the sauce thickens and coats the back of the spoon.

Remove from heat and add the liqueur.

APRICOT TOFFEE PUDDING

Preparation time: 20 minutes

Pressure cooking time: 40 to 45 minutes

Pressure release: Quick release water method

150g (5oz) dried
   apricots, chopped

1 teaspoon bicarbonate soda

70g (2½oz) butter

250g (8oz) brown sugar or honey

2 eggs

Zest of 1 lemon

1 tablespoon vanilla extract

1¼ cups (375g, ¾lb) self-raising
   flour (see Dessert Basics)

Choc toffee sauce (see Dessert
   Basics)

Mix the chopped apricots and bicarb soda with 300ml (10fl oz) boiling water. Soak until the apricots are soft.

Beat butter and sugar until light and pale. Add eggs one at a time, beating well after each one. Add zest and vanilla, beat well.

Puree apricot mixture and fold into the butter mixture, then fold in the flour until combined.

Pour into a lined pudding tin. Attach the lid or cover the soufflé with baking paper. Allow the pudding to rest for 5 minutes before cooking.

Place the trivet in the bottom of the pressure cooker. Pour in enough water so that it just covers the trivet. Place the stainless steel steaming tray on top, followed by the pudding. Lock the lid in place.

Stovetop: Apply medium to high heat to achieve the seal and allow pressure to build up. Once high pressure is reached, turn to low heat and cook pudding for 40 to 45 minutes.

Electric: Turn to medium pressure and cook for 25 to 30 minutes.

Use the quick release water method or quick release lever to release the pressure.

Check if it is cooked by inserting a skewer into the centre. It should come out clean. If not, replace the lid and let it sit there for another 10 minutes.

Pour over toffee sauce and serve.

THE BEST RICE PUDDING WITH CARAMEL APPLES

Preparation time:	10 minutes
Pressure cooking time:	4 minutes
Pressure release:	Natural release method
Resting time:	15 minutes

1L (2 pints) full cream milk
100g (3½oz) honey
1 teaspoon cinnamon
2 tablespoons vanilla extract
½ cup (4oz) sultanas
½ cup (4oz) dried cranberries
2 cups (500g, 1lb) thoroughly
    washed sushi rice, calrose or any
    short grain rice

CARAMEL APPLES
3 tablespoons unsalted butter
3 tablespoons brown sugar
6 unpeeled Pink Lady or Granny
    Smith apples, diced
Juice of ½ a lemon

Almond croissant, to serve
Mascarpone cheese, to serve

Slowly bring the milk, honey, spice, vanilla, sultanas and cranberries to the boil in the pressure cooker. Stir through washed rice and bring to a slow boil. Lock the lid in place.

Stovetop: Apply medium to high heat to achieve the seal and allow pressure to build up. Once low pressure is reached, turn to low heat and cook for 4 minutes.

Electric: Turn to high pressure and cook for 4 minutes.

Use the natural release method to slowly release the pressure.

Slowly sizzle butter in a sauté pan. Add sugar until the sugar starts to caramelise. Add apples and slowly reduce for 5 to 7 minutes on medium heat. Season with lemon juice.

Carefully remove the lid and stir through caramel apple. Allow the rice pudding to rest for 5 minutes before serving.

Serve on a lightly toasted almond croissant with the rice pudding, caramelised apples and a dollop of mascarpone cheese.

CARAMEL FIG AND PORT PUDDING

Preparation time: 15 minutes
Pressure cooking time: 45 to 50 minutes
Pressure release: Quick release water method

300g (10oz) dried figs, chopped
1 teaspoon bicarbonate soda
2 teaspoons ground cinnamon
1¾ cup (420ml, 15oz)
 port, simmering
150g (5oz) soft unsalted butter
1½ cups (300g, 10oz)
 brown sugar
1 teaspoon vanilla essence
3 eggs
2 cups (500g, 1lb) self-raising flour
 (see Dessert Basics)

Combine chopped fig, soda, cinnamon and simmering port in a mixing bowl. Let stand for 20 minutes.

Beat butter and sugar until pale and creamy. Add vanilla and eggs, one at a time. Beat well between each egg.

Fold through fig mixture until well blended. Fold through sifted self-raising flour.

Line a suitable soufflé dish with baking paper. Pour mixture in and cover with more baking paper. Allow the pudding to rest for 5 minutes before cooking.

Stovetop: Pressure cook on a stainless steel steaming tray for 45 to 50 minutes.

Electric: Turn to medium pressure and cook for 25 to 30 minutes.

Use the quick release water method or quick release lever to release the pressure.

Drizzle with caramel sauce to serve (see Dessert Basics).

CHRISTMAS FRUIT AND NUT PUDDING

Preparation time:	30 minutes
Marinating time:	24 hours
Pressure cooking time:	1 hour, 45 minutes
Pressure release:	Quick release water method

MARINATED FRUIT

350g (12oz) mixed dried fruit

150g (5oz) assorted glacé fruit,
roughly chopped

1/3 cup (70g, 1¾oz) brandy

1 tablespoon vanilla essence

PUDDING BASE

250g (8oz) unsalted butter

1¼ cup (250g, 8oz) packed
brown sugar

4 x 55g (1½oz) eggs

1 cup (250g, 8oz) plain flour
plus ½ teaspoon bicarbonate
soda, sifted

½ teaspoon ground cinnamon

½ teaspoon ground ginger

½ teaspoon ground all-spice

1 teaspoon vanilla

½ cup (125g, 4oz)
roasted almonds

½ cup (125g, 4oz)
roasted hazelnuts

½ cup (125g, 4oz) dark chocolate
pieces, roughly chopped

To make the marinated fruit, place all ingredients in a zip-lock bag for a minimum of 12 hours.

Beat butter and sugar until smooth and creamy. Beat in eggs, one at a time, with a tablespoon of flour (this will keep the volume of the butter and sugar stable and prevent the mixture splitting).

Mix in the rest of the flour, spices, vanilla, nuts and chocolate pieces. Fold through the marinated fruit.

Pour into prepared pudding tin and tap a few times to remove any trapped air. Attach lid. Allow the pudding to rest for 5 minutes before cooking.

Fill the pressure cooker with enough water so it touches the top of the trivet and steaming tray. Lock the lid in place.

Stovetop: Apply medium to high heat to achieve the seal and allow pressure to build up. Once high pressure is reached, turn to low heat and cook for 1 hour and 45 minutes.

Electric: Turn to low pressure and cook for 1 hour and 45 minutes.

Use the quick release water method or quick release lever to release the pressure.

Remove and rest the pudding. Serve with brandy custard sauce (see Dessert Basics).

ORANGE AND POPPY SEED PUDDING

Preparation time: 15 minutes
Pressure cooking time: 45 to 50 minutes
Pressure release: Quick release water method

280g (10oz) self-raising flour
  (see Dessert Basics)
1 teaspoon bicarbonate soda
Pinch of salt
80g (3oz) soft butter
3 tablespoons orange marmalade
100g (3½oz) brown sugar
2 eggs, beaten
20g (¾oz) orange zest (1 whole
  navel orange)
2 tablespoons poppy seeds
50ml (1½fl oz) orange juice
2 tablespoons raw vanilla sugar
Lightly whipped cream, to serve

Sift flour, bicarbonate soda and salt into a large mixing bowl.
In a separate bowl, whip butter, marmalade and sugar
until creamy.

Add eggs, one at a time, and then orange zest. Beat
in flour, poppy seeds, juice and vanilla sugar. Pour into a
pudding bowl and attach the lid. Allow the pudding to rest for
5 minutes before cooking.

Add enough water to just touch the trivet and steaming
tray. Place the pudding on the steaming tray. Lock the lid
in place.

Stovetop: Apply medium to high heat to achieve the
seal and allow pressure to build up. Once high pressure is
reached, turn to low heat and cook for 45 minutes.

Electric: Turn to medium pressure and cook for
25 to 30 minutes.

Use the quick release water method or quick release lever
to release the pressure and remove the cake.

Rest cake until it has cooled. Turn pudding out.

Serve warm or cold with lightly whipped cream.

STICKY DATE PUDDING WITH BUTTERSCOTCH

Preparation time:	20 minutes
Pressure cooking time:	50 minutes
Pressure release:	Quick release water method

200g (7oz) pitted dates,
  roughly chopped
1 teaspoon bicarbonate soda
60g (2oz) soft butter
¾ cup (80g, 3oz) caster sugar
2 eggs
1 cup (250g, 8oz) self-raising flour,
  sifted (see Dessert Basics)
100g (3½oz) dark
  chocolate pieces
½ cup (125g, 4oz)
  walnuts, chopped
½ teaspoon ground nutmeg

Place dates in 300ml (10fl oz) boiling water. Remove from the heat, stir in soda, and stand for 5 minutes. Puree date mixture until smooth.

Cream butter and caster sugar. Add eggs, one at a time, and beat well. Fold in flour, then the date puree, chocolate pieces, walnuts and nutmeg. Pour the mixture into a lined pudding tin or soufflé dish.

Allow the pudding to rest for 5 minutes before cooking.

Fill the pressure cooker with enough water to just reach underneath the trivet and stainless steel steaming tray. Bring the water to a rolling boil. Place pudding tin on the steaming tray and lock the lid in place.

Stovetop: Apply medium heat to achieve the seal and allow pressure to build up. Once high pressure is reached, turn to low heat and cook for 45 to 50 minutes.

Electric: Turn to medium pressure and cook for 25 to 30 minutes.

Remove pressure with the quick water method or quick release lever.

Remove the pudding and allow it to cool before serving. Serve with rich butterscotch sauce (see Dessert Basics).

BANANA BLUEBERRY BREAD

Preparation time:	15 minutes
Pressure cooking time:	45 to 50 minutes
Pressure release:	Quick release water method

280g (10oz) self-raising flour
  (see Dessert Basics)
¼ teaspoon bicarbonate soda
1 teaspoon ground cinnamon
1 teaspoon ground nutmeg
80g (3oz) salted soft butter
100g (3½oz) dark brown sugar
2 eggs, beaten
1½ ripe bananas, mashed
1 cup (250g, 8oz) fresh or
  frozen blueberries
¼ cup (60g, 2oz) vanilla sugar

Sift flour, bicarbonate soda, cinnamon and nutmeg into a large mixing bowl.

In a separate bowl, cream butter and sugar until smooth and pale.

Add eggs, one at a time, with a tablespoon of sifted flour. Fold in the rest of the flour, followed by mashed banana, blueberries and vanilla sugar.

Pour the mixture in a prepared pudding tin or soufflé dish. Allow the pudding to rest for 5 minutes before cooking.

Place the trivet on the bottom of the pressure cooker and fill with enough water to just cover the trivet. Place the steaming tray on the trivet, then the pudding tin on top. Lock the lid in place.

Stovetop: Apply medium to high heat to achieve the seal and allow pressure to build up. Once high pressure is reached, turn to low heat and cook for 45 to 50 minutes.

Electric: Turn to medium pressure and cook for 25 to 30 minutes.

Release the pressure using the quick release water method or quick release lever.

Carefully remove the pudding. Allow to cool before serving.

BREAD AND BUTTER PUDDING WITH CROISSANTS AND BANANA

Preparation time:	15 minutes
Pressure cooking time:	45 to 50 minutes
Pressure release:	Quick release water method

3 eggs, beaten

150ml (5fl oz) cream

2 teaspoons vanilla extract

Pinch of nutmeg

Pinch of cinnamon

2 honeycomb chocolate
  bars, crushed

3 croissants, thinly sliced into
  thirds lengthwise

2 ripe bananas, split in half, cut in
  half sideways

2/3 cup (165g, 5½oz) raisins

Vanilla ice-cream, to serve

Prepare pudding tin or soufflé dish with baking paper. Whip eggs, cream, vanilla and spices together for the custard mixture.

Sprinkle 2 tablespoons of crushed honeycomb bar on the bottom of the pudding tin.

Apply a layer of croissant, filling in all the gaps. Pour in one-third of the custard, followed by banana and raisins. Repeat 3 times, gently pressing pudding down so the custard soaks through each layer.

Place a trivet on the bottom of the pressure cooker. Fill with enough water to just cover the trivet. Place the stainless steel steaming tray on top and rest the pudding tin on the steaming tray.Lock the lid in place.

Stovetop: Apply medium to high heat to achieve the seal and allow pressure to build up. Once high pressure is reached, turn to low heat and cook for 45 to 50 minutes.

Electric: Turn to medium pressure and cook for 25 to 30 minutes.

Use the quick release water method or quick release lever to release the pressure. Carefully remove the pudding and allow it to cool slightly.

Serve with vanilla ice-cream.

CHOCOLATE AND RASPBERRY SELF-SAUCING PUDDING

Preparation time:	20 minutes
Pressure cooking time:	45 to 50 minutes
Pressure release:	Quick release water method

350g (12oz) self-rising flour (see
  Dessert Basics), with an extra
  pinch of baking soda added
½ cup (125g, 4oz) caster sugar
½ cup (125g, 4oz) cocoa powder
300g (10oz) dark
  chocolate, grated
1½ cups (360ml, 12fl oz) buttermilk
100g (3½oz) unsalted
  butter, melted
3 eggs, beaten
1 teaspoon pure vanilla essence
1½ cups (360g, 12oz) raspberries
  (or any berry you prefer)

CHOCOLATE SAUCY TOPPING
150g (5oz) brown sugar
2 tablespoons Dutch cocoa powder
  (more intense chocolate flavour)
100ml (3½fl oz) fresh
  espresso coffee

Sift flour, caster sugar, cocoa powder and grated chocolate together into a large mixing bowl.

Add buttermilk, melted butter, beaten eggs and vanilla and whisk well. Gently fold in fruit. Pour into pudding tin lined with baking paper.

Whisk together brown sugar, cocoa powder, ¾ cup (180ml, 6fl oz) boiling water and espresso coffee to a smooth and creamy texture. Drizzle the topping on top of the pudding.

Allow the pudding to rest for 5 minutes before cooking. Lock the lid in place.

Stovetop: Apply medium to high heat to achieve the seal and allow pressure to build up. Once high pressure is reached, turn to low heat and cook for 45 to 50 minutes.

Electric: Turn to medium pressure and cook for 25 to 30 minutes.

Use the quick release water method or quick release lever to release the pressure.

Carefully remove and rest the pudding for 5 minutes before serving. Serve hot.

LEMON CHEESECAKE

Preparation time:	35 minutes
Pressure cooking time:	45 to 50 minutes
Pressure release:	Natural release method

BASE MIXTURE
70g (2½oz) melted butter
150g (5oz) plain sweet
  biscuits, crushed

CHEESECAKE MIXTURE
500g (1lb) soft cream cheese
¾ cup (150g, 5oz) caster sugar
1 tablespoon cornflour
3 eggs
2 tablespoons lemon juice, plus
  zest of 1 lemon
1 tablespoon vanilla essence
Pinch salt

Fresh strawberries, to serve
Whipped cream, to serve

Mix the melted butter and crushed biscuits to form the base.

Press base mixture to the bottom of a lined soufflé dish. Use a potato masher to press the base firmly.

In a food processor, whip cream cheese and sugar until creamy.

While the motor is still running, add cornflour, then one egg at a time. Season with lemon juice, zest, vanilla and a pinch of salt.

Pour mixture into prepared soufflé dish. Cover the top with baking paper.

Fill the pressure cooker with just enough water to reach underneath the trivet and stainless steel steaming tray. Bring the water to a rolling boil. Place the cheesecake on the steaming tray. Lock the lid in place.

Stovetop: Apply medium heat to achieve the seal and allow pressure to build up. Once high pressure is reached, turn to low heat and cook for 45 to 50 minutes.

Electric: Turn to medium pressure and cook for 25 to 30 minutes.

Remove the pressure cooker from the heat and use the natural release method for 15 minutes. Remove any excess pressure with the quick release water method or quick release lever.

Carefully remove the cake. Allow to cool overnight in the fridge until it sets. Top with fresh sliced strawberries and whipped cream.

VANILLA APPLE SPONGE PUDDING

Preparation time: 15 minutes
Pressure cooking time: 45 to 50 minutes
Pressure release: Quick release water method

CARAMELISED APPLE
3 Pink Lady or Granny Smith apples,
    finely cubed
100g (3½oz) brown sugar
50g (1½oz) butter

PUDDING
5 tablespoons golden syrup
175g (6oz) self-raising flour (see
    Dessert Basics), plus 1 teaspoon
    baking powder, sifted 3 times
2 teaspoons real vanilla extract
175g (6oz) unsalted butter,
    room temperature
3 eggs, beaten

CUSTARD CREAM
150ml (5fl oz) soft whipped
    cream, folded into 1 cup
    (250ml, 8fl oz) store-bought or
    homemade custard

To make the caramelised apple, place all ingredients in a sauté pan and slowly braise for 20 minutes.

Squirt golden syrup on the bottom of a lined soufflé dish or pudding tin. Combine sifted flour, caramelised apple, vanilla, butter and beaten eggs. Mix with a rubber spatula.

Pour mixture into prepared soufflé dish and top with baking paper. Allow the pudding to rest for 5 minutes before cooking.

Place a trivet on the bottom of the pressure cooker. Fill with enough water to just cover the trivet. Place the stainless steel steaming tray on top and rest the soufflé dish on it. Lock the lid on.

Stovetop: Apply medium heat to achieve the seal and allow pressure to build up. Once high pressure is reached, turn to low heat and cook for 45 to 50 minutes.

Electric: Turn to medium pressure and cook for 25 to 30 minutes.

Use the quick release water method or quick release lever to release the pressure.

Carefully remove the pudding from the cooker and rest before handling. Serve with custard cream.

INDEX OF RECIPES

ACKNOWLEDGEMENTS

I wish to acknowledge my publisher, Diane Jardine from New Holland Publishing, for giving me the opportunity to write my first book—an unfulfilled aspiration of mine for many years. Thank you for sending me that first email!

Also thanks to project editor Talina McKenzie for expertly guiding me through the writing process and keeping me on track with tight deadlines.

To Shaun Atherstone of Dear Rabbit Photography, Perth for his skill and patience while shooting my portrait photos.

And finally to Chantal Roger, who shares my enthusiasm for pressure cooking and has welcomed me into her Pressure Cooker Centre in Perth to present cooking classes for the past ten years. The seed for this book was planted all those years ago!

You have all contributed to making my writing debut a memorable and rewarding experience.

ABOUT THE AUTHOR

Dale migrated from the USA with his Australian spouse in 1981. He quickly settled into the Sydney food scene, taking over as head chef in a little bistro near Bondi.

He travelled to Perth, Western Australia in 1983 where he set up a freelance chef business called Dial-A-Chef, providing a professional chef service to the restaurant industry. Experiencing first hand the ups and downs of the restaurant business, he saw the need for consulting in restaurants and cafes and now has a large market base built up over 15 years.

Today he is primarily involved in developing recipes for food retailers, teaching kids through an in school food and cooking program and is chief judge at the Perth Royal Show. He also raises funds for the Breast Cancer Council of WA through corporate sponsorship.

First published in 2011 by
New Holland Publishers (Australia) Pty Ltd

Sydney • Auckland • London • Cape Town

1/66 Gibbes Street Chatswood NSW 2067 Australia
218 Lake Road Northcote Auckland New Zealand
86 Edgware Road LondonW2 2EA United Kingdom
80 McKenzie Street Cape Town 8001 South Africa

National Library of Australia Cataloguing-in-Publication Data:

Pressure cooker cookbook / Dale Sniffen.

ISBN: 9781742571423 (pbk.)

1. Pressure cooking.

641.587

Publisher: Diane Jardine
Publishing manager: Lliane Clarke
Project editor: Talina McKenzie
Proofreader: Nina Paine
Designer: Emma Gough
Food photography: Paul Nelson
Photography pp 21, 56–57, 77, 78, 82, 83, 88–89, 116, 117, 126, 127, 147, 168: Graeme
Gillies; pp 5, 16–17, 44–45, 68–69, 82–83, 110–111, 138–139: Emma Gough
Author photo by Shaun Atherstone
Chef/Food stylist: Amanda Luck
Food stylist: Elly Clavell
Production manager: Olga Dementiev
Printer: Toppan Leefung Printing Limited (China)

The publishers would like to thank Breville Australia for assistance on this book.